THE CRUCIBLE

Politics, Property, and Pretense

TWAYNE'S MASTERWORK STUDIES

Robert Lecker, General Editor

THE CRUCIBLE

Politics, Property, and Pretense

James J. Martine

TWAYNE PUBLISHERS
An Imprint of Simon & Schuster Macmillan
New York

Prentice Hall International
London • *Mexico City* • *New Delhi* • *Singapore* • *Sydney* • *Toronto*

Twayne's Masterworks Studies No. 115

The Crucible: Politics, Property, and Pretense
James J. Martine

Twayne Publishers
An Imprint of Simon & Schuster Macmillan
866 Third Avenue
New York, New York 10022

Library of Congress Cataloging-in-Publication Data

Martine, James J.
    The Crucible: politics, property, and pretense / James J. Martine.
        p.   cm. — (Twayne's masterwork studies; no. 115)
    Includes bibliographical references and index.
    ISBN 0-8057-8096-3 — ISBN 0-8057-8584-1 (pbk.)
    1. Miller, Arthur, 1915–   Crucible. 2. Politics and literature-United States—History—20th century. 3. Salem (Mass.) in literature. 4. Witchcraft in literature.
I. Title. II. Series.
PS3525.I5156C735 1993
812'.52—dc20   93-2843
                                                                                      CIP

The paper used in this publication meets the minimum requirements of American National Standard for Information Sciences—Permanence of Paper for Printed Library Materials. ANSI Z3948-1984. ⊗™

10 9 8 7 6 5 4 3 2 1 (hc)
10 9 8 7 6 5 4 3 2   (pb)

Printed in the United States of America

This book is for Alyce Sands Miller

Contents

Note on the References
and Acknowledgments

Quotations from the text of *The Crucible* throughout this monograph refer to the most readily available paperback edition (New York: Penguin Books, 1976), and page numbers are included parenthetically in the citations.

After more than two decades of teaching the works of Arthur Miller in university classrooms, I cannot properly acknowledge my indebtedness to the perceptivity and insights of the scholars of Miller's works who have come before me or my debt to the energy and enthusiasm of a generation of undergraduate students. My gratitude to those scholars whose works I have drawn upon; where possible I have acknowledged my debts. Further, I would be remiss if I were not to recognize the importance of *Timebends* as the most thorough, convenient, and current compendium of Miller's thought. My reading of the play, however, and the responsibility for that reading, are mine alone.

The frontispiece sketch of the dramatist comes from my private collection, was commissioned for this volume, and is reproduced here with the permission of the artist, Peg Bothner. My thanks to her and to Gene Feist, artistic director, and the Roundabout Theatre Company for the photographs that appear in this volume with their permission. Thanks as well to my daughter Stephanie Martini Papoulis, a member of the Roundabout Theatre's Ensemble Company, for her assistance in acquiring the photos. Further thanks to Joan Fox, the Chautauqua Institution, and the Chautauqua Opera for the photograph of their production of Ward's opera *The Crucible* reproduced here with their permission. Finally, thanks to the opera's composer, Robert Ward, for his generous cooperation during an informative interview.

My gratitude to reference librarians Theresa Shaffer, Ardythe Nothem, and James Lee; to Carol Diminnie, Dean of Graduate Studies and the St. Bonaventure University Research Council for their support; to Professors Leo E. Keenan and Joseph S. Tedesco for their intelligence and understanding; to Tom Chapman for his encouragement; and to Lawrence D. Ford, university director of personnel and management services, for the bread and water he brought up to the ivory tower during the final three months of composition.

Illustrations

Arthur Miller
Sketch by Peg Bothner. Courtesy of the artist

Chronology:
Arthur Miller's Life and Works

1915   Arthur Asher Miller born 17 October on 112th Street in New York City to father, Isidore, who is successful in garment industry, and mother, Augusta, who teaches public school. Arthur is second of three children (older brother Kermit and younger sister Joan, who becomes the actress Joan Copeland).

1928   Father's business declines; family moves to Midwood section of Brooklyn. Attends James Madison High School for a full term before graduation from grammar school.

1932   Graduates from Abraham Lincoln High School; applications to Cornell and University of Michigan both rejected. Works very briefly in garment industry. Writes first story, "In Memoriam," depicting situation of an aging salesman. Works as shipping clerk in automobile parts warehouse on Tenth Avenue in Manhattan for more than a year at $15 per week. Discovers serious literature, including Dostoyevski's *The Brothers Karamazov.* Reapplies to University of Michigan and is granted conditional acceptance in journalism.

1934   Enrolls at University of Michigan; to support himself, washes dishes in cafeteria and earns small salary as night editor of *Michigan Daily.*

1936   First play, *No Villain,* produced at Michigan and wins university's Avery Hopwood Award.

1937   Playwriting class with Professor Kenneth T. Rowe. *No Villain,* revised and retitled *They Too Arise,* earns prize from the Theatre Guild Bureau of New Plays. *Honors at Dawn* wins a Hopwood Award.

1938	Graduates in June with B.A. in English. Moves back to New York; writes scripts for Federal Theatre Project.
1940	Marries college sweetheart, Mary Grace Slattery. They will have two children, Robert and Jane. Sells to prestigious Columbia Workshop his first radio play, a political satire called "The Pussycat and the Expert Plumber Who Was a Man." Holds variety of jobs, from truckdriver to steamfitter at Brooklyn Navy Yard.
1944	Tours army camps for background material for *The Story of G. I. Joe,* a screenplay based on Ernie Pyle's *Here Is Your War.* Publishes journal of Army camp tour as *Situation Normal.* 23 November, *The Man Who Had All the Luck* premieres at Forrest Theatre; his first play on Broadway runs four performances, loses $55,000.
1945	*Focus,* a novel drawn from his exposure to anti-Semitism, is published.
1945–1946	Struggles with a drama then called "The Sign of the Archer"; discouraged, he considers abandoning the theater.
1947	After six drafts, the play is produced 29 January 1947 as *All My Sons* and runs for 328 performances. Three months after opening, the New York Drama Critics bypass Eugene O'Neill's *The Iceman Cometh* to award *All My Sons* their annual Circle Award; by May, it sees productions in Paris and Stockholm and, along with *Focus,* is purchased for motion pictures. Miller's reputation as a playwright is established.
1948	Completes working draft of "The Inside of His Head."
1949	This play, retitled *Death of a Salesman,* opens 10 February at the Morosco Theatre in New York after a highly successful engagement in Philadelphia; it runs for 742 performances, until November 1950. *Salesman* receives, among other awards, the Pulitzer Prize and the Antoinette Perry Award.
1950	In Hollywood briefly, Miller meets Marilyn Monroe; occasional but warm correspondence follows. A month after *Salesman* closes, Miller's adaptation of Henrik Ibsen's *An Enemy of the People* opens (28 December), but folds after 36 performances.
1953	*The Crucible* opens 22 January at Martin Beck Theatre, runs for 197 performances, and wins both Antoinette Perry and Donaldson awards as best play of the year; original cast includes Arthur Kennedy as Proctor, E. G. Marshall as Hale,

Beatrice Straight as Elizabeth, and Walter Hampden as Danforth.

1954   Miller is denied a passport by the State Department to go to Brussels to attend the Belgian premiere of *The Crucible,* under regulations refusing passports to persons believed to be supporting the Communist movement. The move is considered retaliation because *The Crucible* invites comparisons between the Salem witch trials and McCarthy-era communist witch-hunt hysteria.

1955   Marilyn Monroe moves to New York City. 29 September: *A View from the Bridge* and *A Memory of Two Mondays* (one-act plays) open at Coronet Theatre in New York to the bleakest critical reception of a Miller work since his first play; they run for a disappointing 149 performances. Miller is charged with left-wing activities by Scripps-Howard reporter Frederick Woltman in the *New York World-Telegram* and is investigated by New York City Youth Board for possible communist associations.

1956   Receives honorary doctorate from University of Michigan. On 21 June, testifies before House Un-American Activities Committee; refuses to name persons seen at meetings organized by communist sympathizers. On 12 June, marriage to Mary Slattery ends in Reno divorce; marries Marilyn Monroe in civil ceremony on 27 June and again in Jewish service on 1 July. On 10 July is cited for contempt of Congress by a vote of 373 to 9. Two-act version of *A View from the Bridge* opens in London on 11 October.

1957   In February, indicted on two charges of contempt; trial concludes on 23 May with Miller found guilty on both counts. On 19 July he is fined $500 and given a suspended one-month jail sentence; appeals. *Collected Plays* published.

1958   On 8 April, nine-man U.S. court of appeals reverses contempt of Congress conviction. Elected to National Institute of Arts and Letters.

1959   Awarded institute's Gold Medal for Drama.

1961   Screenplay for film *The Misfits.* Divorces Marilyn Monroe.

1962   Marries Inge Morath on 17 February; daughter Rebecca born 18 months later. Death of Marilyn Monroe on 5 August.

1964   *After the Fall* premieres 23 January; *Incident at Vichy* premieres 3 December; both plays produced for the Lincoln

Center Repertory Company at the ANTA-Washington Square Theatre in New York City.

1965   Elected to four-year term as president of P.E.N., international literary association. London production of *The Crucible* produced for the National Theatre by Laurence Olivier, starring Colin Blakely and Joyce Redman; Miller calls it the best staging of the play he has seen.

1967   Publishes collection of short stories, *I Don't Need You Anymore*. 4 May, television version of *The Crucible*, starring George C. Scott and Colleen Dewhurst, specially adapted by Miller.

1968   On 7 February, *The Price* opens at Morosco Theatre. Miller is delegate to Democratic National Convention in Chicago.

1969   Publishes travel journal *In Russia*, text accompanying photographs by Inge Morath.

1971   *The Portable Arthur Miller* published.

1972   *The Creation of the World and Other Business* opens 30 November at Shubert Theatre and closes after 20 performances. Delegate to Democratic National Convention in Miami.

1974   *Up from Paradise*, a musical version of *The Creation of the World and Other Business*, with book, lyrics, and direction by Miller, is presented in Ann Arbor 23 April by the University of Michigan Theatre Programs.

1977   Publishes *In the Country*, text accompanying photographs by Inge Morath. *The Archbishop's Ceiling* produced at the Kennedy Center for the Performing Arts, Washington, D.C.

1978   *The Theater Essays of Arthur Miller* published. Leaves Paris to attend twenty-fifth anniversary production of *The Crucible* in Brussels, where he had been forbidden to go by the U.S. State Department in 1954; discovers he has left his passport in France; at reception given in his honor by consul general of U.S. embassy in Belgium, he requests new passport and is issued one the next morning.

1979   Publishes *Chinese Encounters*, text accompanying photographs by Inge Morath.

1980   Adapts Fania Fenelon's book as television screenplay, "Playing for Time," a CBS production on 30 September. *The American Clock* premieres in New York 20 November. Hospitalized several days in Waterbury Hospital Health Center in December with broken leg.

Chronology

1981   *Arthur Miller's Collected Plays, Volume 2* published.

1982   Two one-act plays, *Elegy for a Lady* and *Some Kind of Love Story,* produced 9 November as *2 by A. M.*

1983   In May, fire damages his Roxbury, Connecticut, home. Goes to China to stage *Death of a Salesman* at the Beijing Peoples' Art Theatre.

1984   *Salesman in Beijing* published. Awarded Kennedy Center Honors for distinguished lifetime achievement, and at the opening banquet in the Cannon Office Building he appreciates the irony, pointed out by his friend and lawyer, Joe Rauh, of Miller's being honored in the same room in which his House Un-American Activities Committee hearing had been held 28 years earlier.

1985   Begins writing his autobiography.

1986   Two one-act plays, *I Can't Remember Anything* and *Clara,* published as *Danger: Memory!;* produced in New York 8 February 1987.

1987   Publication of autobiography, *Timebends: A Life.*

1989   Major revival of *The Crucible,* directed by Arvin Brown, 21 November to 7 January 1990 at Long Wharf Theatre in New Haven, with Frank Converse as Proctor.

1990   Screenplay for motion picture *Everybody Wins;* revival of *The Crucible,* 14 March through 13 May, at Roundabout Theatre Company, New York, with Randle Mell as Proctor and Justine Bateman as Abigail; revival of *The Crucible* at National Theatre in London, with Tom Wilkinson as Proctor; revival of *The Crucible* by the National Actors Theatre, New York, 8 November 1991–5 January 1992, with Martin Sheen as Proctor.

1991   World premiere of *The Ride Down Mt. Morgan* at Wyndham's Theatre, London on 31 October 1991; play closes after three months.

1993   *The Last Yankee*, a comedy-drama, has its world premiere at the Manhattan Theatre Club. Previews begin 5 January 1993 and limited engagement runs 21 January 1993 to 28 February 1993.

LITERARY AND HISTORICAL CONTEXT

GENERAL AND HISTORICAL
CONTEXT

1.

Matrices: Distant and Near

Since *The Crucible* is both a historical play and a parable about the political and social witch-hunts of the time of its composition, there are, in fact, two historical contexts against which it may be seen—seventeenth-century colonial America and the United States of the 1950s. Miller had known about the events at Salem since his undergraduate days, but it was the mid-twentieth century anticommunist paranoia that compelled him to drive alone on a cold spring day in 1952 from his home in New York City to the then little-known Salem Historical Society in Massachusetts to begin his research on the Salem witchcraft trials. New England cases of witchcraft, and the subsequent trials and executions—the very stuff of Miller's finished drama—are now fairly well known, but they need to be seen in perspective.

It might be helpful to remind ourselves at how great a distance in time from us the prototypes of Miller's characters existed. The setting of the play is in the spring of 1692, a year in the minds of the people of Salem when God and the Devil wrestled for control of their community. Seventeenth-century society believed unequivocally in a dualistic universe, a world of matter and the flesh and an invisible world of the spirit. The Puritans, who had arrived in 1620, were the dominant group of New England settlers. Martin Luther had died as recently as 1546 and, more to the point for the Puritans, John Calvin had died in 1564. Their past and heritage were not all that distant—not as distant as their world was from that of the 1950s.

Generally speaking, the stereotype of the Puritan as a sour-faced champion of rigid morality is misleading and inaccurate. On the whole, the Puritans of Massachusetts contributed more good to this nation's evolution than harm. The most significant aspects of the Puritan legacy would include strong feelings for democracy, enthusiasm for education, a fervor for social reform, and a lingering awareness that, despite an emphasis on material success, the pursuit of financial gain is not sufficient as a major goal in life. Yet, perversely, the most fixed image of this group for the popular imagination may have been derived from the extreme zealots who did in fact, once led to the brink of hysterical superstition, persecute "witches." It is true that well-meaning and well-trained seventeenth-century clergymen were powerful temporal as well as spiritual forces in their time, a time struggling against a coming Enlightenment; under the encroachment of secular influences, their civil powers had begun to crumble to such a degree that they may have felt a need to reassert their waning authority. When Reverend Samuel Parris cries out to his niece Abigail that he has "fought here three long years to bend these stiff-necked people to me" (11), Miller not only allows his audience access to Parris's paranoid character, but also provides a brief articulation of historical evolution. Yet, despite all that, it may be possible to understand, in part, what happened at Salem by coming to an understanding of the quite real power of witchcraft upon a society that profoundly— if not without exception—believed in the reality of magic, witches, spells, and the powerful efficacy of witchcraft.

The events that occurred at Salem were odious, but are dwarfed by the terrifying specter of the executions that took place simultaneously abroad. No more than 50 people were executed in New England, less than 30 if one were to exclude the cause célèbre of Salem. The execution of 20 "witches" seems no minor matter when seen from a distance of 300 years, but it looks different when one compares it to the many thousands of people who were burned as witches in Europe. (Witches were burned on the Continent, where witchcraft was a heresy, and hanged in England and New England, where witchcraft was a felony.) Thus the trials at Salem and the concomitant executions were not unique, nor were they the most egregious human-rights violations of their time.

What was it, then, about the situation of the Salem trials specifically that inspired Miller and so served his muse? First of all, it has been often said of the New England Puritans that there never existed a group of people who were so sure they were right. Many of them felt free to act precisely because they had no doubts about the justice and righteousness of their cause. To them, civil laws and the laws of God were nearly the same thing; consequently, they allowed no dissent. It was this moral absolutism that at once appalled and interested Miller and that he would use to connect 1692 Salem with the hearings of the House Un-American Activities Committee in Washington in the 1950s. There were other elements in the genesis of the play, to be sure, but more of them later.

What of the specific historical events in Salem that Miller would use as the focus and structural framework of his play? Early in the year 1692, several young girls in Salem Village—now Danvers, Massachusetts—were taken ill and began to display disconcerting symptoms. The girls were Abigail Williams, age 11; Ann Putnam, Jr., 12; Mary Warren, 20; Mercy Lewis, 19; Mary Walcott, 16; Elizabeth Hubbard, 17; and Elizabeth Parris, 9. It will, of course, be immediately evident to the audience of Miller's play that he has, for dramatic purposes, reduced the number of girls involved and adjusted Abigail's age upward. The girls were subject to hallucinations and hysterical seizures, which the village doctor is said to have ascribed to witchcraft being practiced upon them. This situation, fully developed, led to warrants being issued on 29 February 1692 for the slave Tituba, a Carib Indian woman, along with Sarah Good and Sarah Osburn, old women of dubious reputations, and the three were examined on 1 March. Thereafter, events followed quickly. On 4 April complaints were filed against Goodwife Cloyse and Elizabeth Procter (allowing for the idiosyncratic aspect of seventeenth-century spelling, which had not yet been regularized, history's John and Elizabeth Procter become Arthur

Miller's Proctors), who were examined on 11 April. The examination of Giles Corey, Abigail Hobbes, and Bridget Bishop followed on 19 April. On 2 June 1692, Bridget Bishop was sentenced to death; she was hanged eight days later. The trial of Sarah Good, Susannah Martin, Elizabeth Howe, Sarah Wildes, and Rebecca Nurse, the most conspicuously innocent person, was held on 30 June; all five were executed on 19 July.

The witchcraft hysteria, now apparently fed by the town's paranoia, jealousies, and animosities, raged out of control. On 23 July Elizabeth Procter's husband, John, wrote a letter to five eminent Boston clergymen in the hope that they would intercede with Governor William Phips on behalf of the Salem victims. His plea was ineffectual. On 11 April, Procter had been committed to prison in Boston, even though his residence was in Salem Farms. This change of locale may have been necessitated because thirty-two of Procter's local friends and neighbors had signed a petition for his reprieve.

Six people went to trial on 5 August 1692: George Burroughs, John Willard, George Jacobs, Sr., Martha Carrier, and John and Elizabeth Procter. All six were found guilty and all were condemned to death. Since Procter and his wife were both in prison, the sheriff came to their house, seized all the goods and provisions, sold some of the cattle at half price and killed the rest, "threw out the Beer out of a Barrel, and carried away the Barrel; emptied a Pot of Broath, and took away the Pot, and left nothing in the House for the support of the Children."[1] Because Elizabeth Procter was pregnant, she escaped the fate of the others; John Procter and the other four were hanged on 19 August. Nor was that to be the conclusion. On 22 September 1692, Martha Corey, Mary Easty, Alice Parker, Ann Pudeator, Margaret Scott, Wilmot "Mammy" Redd, Samuel Wardwell, and Mary Parker were executed, bringing the total of those hanged to 19.

The final person to lose his life deserves special if brief mention here. In September 1692, Giles Corey, who was over 80 years old, chose to stand mute and not respond to the charges brought against him. Under both British law and the laws of New England, a man who refused to answer could not be tried; he could, however, be tortured until he answered—or died. Corey was pressed, that is, placed upon the ground with gradually increased weight piled on him; it took him two days to die. During the process of the pressing, his "tongue being prest out of his Mouth, the Sheriff with his Cane forced it in again, when he was dying. He was the first in New-England, that was ever prest to Death" (Burr, 367).[2] Because this event plays a large part in act 4 of Miller's drama and John Proctor's final decision, it will be dealt with in detail later.

As quickly as the executions had begun, they were over. In the space of less than 100 days, 20 people had gone to their death. The witch-hunt was over by the time Elizabeth Procter gave birth in January 1693. Shortly thereafter, Governor Phips issued a general pardon, and the inevitable reaction set in. In 1697 Massachusetts established a day of fasting to repent for the innocent blood that had been shed at Salem; in 1699 the members of the Nurse family were welcomed back into communion; and in 1703 the formal sentence of excommunication of Martha Corey was revoked.

This is essentially the historical episode, in brief compass, that Miller had from his research at the Historical Society "Witch Museum." There were, however, other things troubling Miller's mind at this time. The day before he was to leave for the exploratory trip to Salem, Miller received a telephone call from Elia Kazan, a man the playwright loved like a brother. Miller had great respect for both the man and the director Kazan, who had staged *All My Sons* and *Death of a Salesman.* Miller drove to Kazan's home to learn that his friend had been subpoenaed by the House Un-American Activities Committee (HUAC) and had cooperated completely in executive session, naming names of people he had known to be members of the Communist party. Kazan had done this, as others had, to survive in his chosen profession and avoid blacklisting. Those named might not be so fortunate. Miller's anger rose against the HUAC, not his friend—for whom he felt sadness—because it was not Kazan's "duty to be stronger than he was, the government had no right to require anyone to be stronger than it had been given him to be."[3] As Miller resumed his automobile journey to Salem, it was clearly evident that he meant to equate the witches of ancient Salem Village with the pandemic witch-hunt that was then sweeping the nation for the bogeyman of communism.

The peace that had ended World War II brought a conclusion to the clash between the great Allied nations and the powers of fascism, but it saw the beginning of an open conflict between the two major economic systems of the world. To the capitalist world, rushing to enjoy the fruits of the postwar era, the very word *communist* was anathema. Anticommunism became a movement of its own, and everywhere many Americans looked they found cause for alarm. As early as 1947, the Truman Doctrine articulated the attempt to contain the spread of communism and provided aid to noncommunist nations that sought assistance against communist aggression. In March of that year, President Harry Truman announced a program to check the "loyalty" of all U.S. government workers. On 23 September 1949 Truman announced that the Soviet Union had developed and tested an atomic bomb, and a cold shudder passed across the American nation. Hard upon that, on 1 October 1949, the civil war that had been raging in China ended as the nationalist forces under Chiang Kai-shek were driven from the mainland by the communist forces led by Mao Tse-tung and supported by the Soviet bloc; Mao proclaimed the country the People's Republic of China. In 1950 growing tension between the two great political systems of the world disillusioned many Americans about the chances for détente between the communist and noncommunist nations.

Persons passing secret documents to the Soviets and the conviction of Ethel and Julius Rosenberg for conspiring to steal atomic secrets added fuel to the mounting concerns. The existence of the atomic bomb on both sides of the Iron Curtain increased a national fear, which fed the anticommunist fervor. Into the arena at this moment rode a self-proclaimed champion, the man who would give his name to an epoch in American history, Senator Joseph McCarthy of Wisconsin, a strident and voluble anticommunist. At a speaking engagement at the Republican Women's Club of Wheeling, West Virginia, McCarthy claimed he had the names of 205 persons in the U.S. State Department who were members of the Communist party. The fact that a majority of a Senate committee investigating these charges demonstrated that they were a hoax or that eventually, in 1954, the Unites States Senate would censure McCarthy did little to assuage the growing anticommunist hysteria that began to sweep the country.

Nor did the judiciary or international events help matters. On 10 April 1950 the Supreme Court upheld the right of congressional committees to force witnesses to reveal if they were Communists in a case against two film writers, and in June North Korean forces came across the thirty-eighth parallel. The nightmares of many Americans thus came true—there were witches after all, and some of them were our neighbors.

In September 1950, the McCarran International Security Act required that all members of the Communist party register with the Justice Department and all communist-front organizations reveal their membership. In April 1951, Truman declared that federal employees could be dismissed if there were any "reasonable doubt" about their loyalty. By 1952 the Supreme Court had upheld a New York State law banning public-school teachers who might be members of subversive organizations; the McCarran-Walter Act had tightened provisions for the exclusion of aliens who might be risks to the nation's security; and the HUAC hearings had fanned the flames of the national paranoia concerning the Red menace.

Against a backdrop of all this sound and fury, *The Crucible* opened at the Martin Beck Theatre in New York on 22 January 1953, at the peak of the power of what is now called "McCarthyism"; reproach and disgrace, however, were just around the corner for the Republican senator from Wisconsin. McCarthy eventually entertained millions of Americans watching the televised investigation of the U.S. Army during the summer of 1954. On 24 August the Communist Control Act outlawed the Communist party and denied certain civil rights to organizations believed to be communist-front. That same year Mrs. Ruth Shipley, head of the Passport Bureau of the State Department, denied Arthur Miller renewal of his passport, which he needed to attend the Brussels premiere of *The Crucible,* and in 1956 Miller himself was questioned by the HUAC.

Ironically, Miller's troubles with the HUAC came after McCarthy himself was censured by a Senate vote of 67 to 22 on 2 December 1954. Although McCarthy remained in the Senate until

1956, his power was effectively curbed by his Senate colleagues, who found his behavior an affront to the Senate's dignity and an obstruction to constitutional processes.

The matrices of Miller's *The Crucible* were events separated by some two hundred and sixty years—but joined in the sense that elements of disparate societies each sought only evidence of guilt and ignored or suppressed all evidence to suggest otherwise. This seems a serviceable if as yet incomplete definition of a witch-hunt.

Miller's play about the events at Salem provided a stark reminder of the dangers of infectious paranoia and suggestible hysterics in a broad social and political setting and struck its own effective blow at McCarthyism.

2

The Importance of the Work

A work of literature is often more highly valued because it is a watershed in the development of its genre or because it has a significant influence on subsequent art and artists. Innovation and influences, however, will not alone provide proper measures of the importance of *The Crucible*. If the play is not *the* great American drama—if it does not hold the high regard in the minds of many American critics that Eugene O'Neill's *Long Day's Journey into Night* does, for example—if it, in fact, is not even widely considered to be Miller's best play, we must point out in all fairness that it has been produced with greater frequency than almost any other American play, including Tennessee Williams's *A Streetcar Named Desire* and Thornton Wilder's *Our Town*. Commercial success and popular reception are not, of course, appropriate or adequate measures of a work's merit, yet there must be a reason for the play's continuing popularity. *The Crucible* is not as innovative in form or experimental in structure as *Death of a Salesman,* but it continues to have a broad readership and a vast audience both at home and abroad—and on both sides of what used to be called the Iron Curtain.

There is little question of the play's importance in Miller's canon. Even if the initial production was, to Miller's way of thinking, less than ideal and the critical reception somewhat mixed, it solidified the playwright's position. Coming as it did directly after *All My Sons, Death of a Salesman,* and Miller's adaptation of Ibsen's *An Enemy of the People,* it confirmed Miller's reputation as one of America's most important and serious playwrights. Only O'Neill and Williams among Americans are mentioned as peers. Whatever the reaction to the play, *The Crucible* assured Miller of an audience thereafter, and thus is important in that respect.

The play's position as social observation, moreover, was significant for those who cherished the earlier theater of the 1930s and saw Miller's effort here as a return of the theater as not merely a place for entertainment or diversion, but a forum where social and political issues could be confronted and explored.

What of the influence of this play upon other drama and dramatists? Is the play in any way a watershed, changing the direction or landscape of the American theater? Miller is said to have had little immediate influence upon subsequent American drama, the sort of influence that Eugène Ionesco and Samuel Beckett had on the manner and matter of later playwrights like David Rabe and Albert Innaurato. Much of the significance of mainstream American drama has been underestimated by scholars and avant-garde critics, some of whom see the style of *The Crucible* as anachronistic. Perhaps at some future time, when Miller's canon has been completed and evaluated in retrospect, the effectiveness of the theater of David Mamet, Lanford Wilson, and August Wilson will call attention to Miller's proper position in the evolution of American drama.

What Miller may be proudest of is that the play's influence may be recognized as more profound in a social or historical context than in a formal or stylistic one.

Miller has never been a dilettante. As a playwright, he is not merely an entertaining host, and his dramas generally are not entertainments. One does not slip casually into a theater to see a Miller play to forget the real world for a few hours. Most significant literature allows its audience to both escape and approach reality at the same time. Miller's genius is more that of approach than escape. For art to be valid for Miller, it must be of use in changing society, and none of his plays is more informed by this didactic principle or revolutionary purpose than *The Crucible*. Miller's didacticism is never preachy—often it is so much a part of the warp and woof of the rich tapestry woven into his drama as to be indiscernible to all but the most practiced eye or alert ear, and most often it is almost impossible to distinguish between his "revolutionary" intent and the more subtle metaphysics of democracy. Curiously, though, he never saw himself as either a revolutionary or a political writer. First and foremost, he considers himself a moralist. If his works are often taken for social commentary, that is not their primary intent.

A crucible is a severe test or a hard trial. More pointedly, the term also refers to a container that can resist great heat and is used for melting and calcining ores; most commonly the end product that comes out of the crucible is a purer high-grade steel. As Danforth quite directly warns Proctor, "it is my duty to tell you this. We burn a hot fire here; it melts down all concealment" (89).

The title obviously, then, refers to the test or hard trial that Proctor undergoes. With all concealment melted down, the product—Proctor's moral constitution—is of a higher quality. On the other hand, we must not overlook the significance of the fact that, as Miller well knew, a crucible is a melting pot—what this nation claims itself to be. Thus, *The Crucible* may be said to stand as a figure for America itself. As such, Miller's play is an examination of America, from its seventeenth-century beginnings to the events of the 1950s. Miller's ambivalent evaluation of the continuity from the Puritans to the present comes to the conclusion that "they believed, in short, that they held in their steady hands the candle that would light the world. We have inherited this belief, and it has helped and hurt us" (5).

When discussing why *The Crucible* is his own favorite of his plays, Miller says,

> first of all, it's the most produced of my plays, more than *Salesman* or anything else. I'm proud of it in the sense that it seems to reach the young very well. They do it all over the place.

And I get very moving letters from them sometimes about where it has sent their minds in relation to liberty, in relation to the rights of people. It seems to affect their living as citizens. Which is terrific. And I kind of feel proud about that. They're stronger in their belief in the best things in America because of that.

Equally, it makes a statement abroad. *The Crucible* . . . when it gets produced in some foreign country, especially in Latin America this has been true, it's either that a dictator is about to arise and take over, or he has just been over-thrown. I'm glad something of mine is useful as a kind of a weapon like that. It speaks for people against tyranny, and that's nothing to be ashamed of.[1]

While the play was at first seen as an allegory about the McCarthy witch-hunt, its real importance could be appreciated only after the initial furor died down. *The Crucible is* about witchcraft at Salem in 1692, and it *was* inspired by the social and political climate in the United States in the 1950s—Miller is the first to admit that—but these specific historical events do not account for the play's continuing popularity throughout the world. At the 1965 National Theatre production of the play in London, for example, Miller overheard a young woman whisper to her escort, "Didn't this have something to do with that American Senator—what was his name?" Miller concedes "that it felt marvellous that McCarthy was what's-his-name while *The Crucible* was *The Crucible* still."[2] Moreover, and perhaps even more to the point, the playwright recalls being greatly affected in 1988 upon meeting Nien Cheng, the 70-year-old author of an account of her six-year imprisonment during China's Cultural Revolution, who, with tears in her eyes, related the play, which she had seen in a Shanghai theater, to her own experience ("Again They Drink," 36). Many people abroad have little or no clue as to who McCarthy was or what McCarthyism was about. One of the resources upon which the play draws, clear to someone with Nien Cheng's experience, may be Miller's contention that "the very idea of authority was fraudulent" (*Timebends,* 552).

Without a broader message, *The Crucible* might have perished in the 1950s or become a historical oddity of interest only to historians of New England and people curious about witchcraft. Since the play transcends both aspects of its historicity, its endurance and effectiveness must be found in other, grander matters. It may be that beyond Salem and beyond the witch-hunts of the 1950s, Miller had touched truths of the human spirit. The play continues to be produced because it addresses matters that are of continuing concern to intelligent men and women. The play possesses themes and underlying universals which apparently transcend time and place, including national borders. It is produced in China, the Soviet Union, continental Europe, and Latin America in addition to England and the United States.

Miller's own estimate suggests that the sun barely sets on this play. Scarcely a week goes by when it is not produced somewhere in the world ("Again They Drink," 36). By Miller's kenning, the importance of this play will not be measured by the number of performances, financial rewards, or theatrical and literary affinities to earlier or later works, but by its influence upon people, young and old, and such impetus as it lends to inspiring "their minds in relation to liberty, in relation to the rights of people."

3

Critical Reception

The Crucible has now reached the status of an American masterwork, as both literature and drama. It is produced, read, discussed, and examined in American colleges and universities. Increasingly taught in high schools as well, the play has developed a large and appreciative audience.

It was not always that way. Miller himself delights in recalling that the American playwright Clifford Odets, author of *Waiting for Lefty* and *Awake and Sing,* once denigrated the play to Elia Kazan as "just a story about a bad marriage" (*Timebends,* 236). This wry comment—by a fellow dramatist from whom Miller felt competitive resentment—aside, the overall critical reception of the play is instructive. One scholar recounts the play's opening thus: "*The Crucible* was first performed at the Martin Beck theatre in New York, on January 22, 1953. The first-night audience received the play tumultuously and enthusiastically, according it 19 curtain calls and insisting that the author appear on the stage to accept in person the shouts of Bravo which echoed throughout the house. An auspicious beginning indeed."[1]

An auspicious beginning indeed, except that this is not quite the way Arthur Miller recalls it. The play *had* received an enthusiastic welcome in Wilmington, Delaware, on its first public performance prior to Broadway, and the audience was standing at the final curtain calling for the play's author. Miller, standing at the back of the house in the company of fellow playwright Lillian Hellman, joined in laughter to see Jed Harris, the play's director—warmly remembered by the playwright for his chutzpah—suddenly come on stage to accept the accolades intended for the author (*Timebends,* 346). Miller's recollection of the play's New York opening is quite something else:

> I have never been surprised by the New York reception of a play, and opening night in the Martin Beck . . . was no exception. I knew we had cooled off a very hot play, which therefore was not going to move anyone very deeply. . . . What I had not bargained for . . . was the hostility in the New York audience as the theme of the play was revealed; an invisible sheet of ice formed over their heads, thick enough to skate on. In the lobby at the end, people with whom I had some fairly close professional acquaintanceships passed me by as though I were invisible. (*Timebends,* 347)

There is some small irony in the fact that Miller's play, which is in part about righteous certainty and moral absolutism, then fell in among New York theater critics—that bastion of absolute certainty. Yet the major critics were, by and large, kind to Miller. The response of the major New York newspaper critics was, simply put, a case of great expectation. After *Death of a Salesman,* they expected every one of his plays to be a masterpiece and their reviews indicate as much.

Walter Kerr, then of the *Herald Tribune,* had high expectations because of the past performances of *All My Sons* and *Death of a Salesman,* and saw *The Crucible* as a step backward. He found the play a mechanical parable and too much of an ideological polemic. Kerr, one of the best of the New York critics, on this occasion was caught up in his review with the contemporary parallels to the latest headlines. Brooks Atkinson, the most influential reviewer of the time, as the drama critic for the *New York Times,* conceded the similarities between the situation of 1953 and that of 1692, but found it another powerful play. Yet Atkinson, to whom Miller felt he owed a great deal for an important reconsideration of *All My Sons* that won the playwright an audience, also had difficulty seeing the indigenous merits of the play because it fell in the shadow of *Death of a Salesman*. Richard Watts of the *New York Post* likewise saw the power of the play, but he, too, felt that the play suffered from the singular fact that it followed upon *Death of a Salesman*.

Other critics, however, were unstinting in their praise of the play, considering it an unqualified triumph. John Chapman in the *Daily News,* Robert Coleman in the *Daily Mirror,* and especially William Hawkins in the *New York World Telegram and Sun,* all taking the play on its own merits, saw the drama as an important advance in Miller's oeuvre. The play ran 197 performances, a disappointment when compared to the 742 performances of *Death of a Salesman* and the 328 performances of *All My Sons,* but it did go on to win both the Antoinette Perry and the Donaldson awards as best play of the year.

The magazine critics, without the deadlines of the New York theater reviewers, had time and space in which to explore the play's analogy to the current hysterical search for subversives. John Mason Brown in the *Saturday Review of Literature,* like the major daily reviewers, said the play lacked the substance of Miller's earlier work, and found the drama too crowded. The reviewer for the *Daily Worker* obviously seized upon parallels between Salem and the communist witch-hunt but curiously saw in the play an overt example of class struggle, which, given the facts of the matter—both in American history and in the play—might have been very difficult to support. The commentator for *Commonweal* dealt with the matters of hysteria and ideology, but quickly cut through all that to point out, quite rightly, that Miller's continuing and representative theme is integrity, and this fact is integral to understanding *The Crucible*.

Perhaps the most celebrated attack on the play was Eric Bentley's review in the *New Republic*. Bentley found Miller's allegory naive and accused the dramatist of being an innocent who seemed not to realize that the menace of communism was real while witches and witchcraft were fictitious. Moreover, Bentley proposed that the play itself was melodrama, in part because the villains were too evil and the heroes too good. One who essentially agrees with this estimation is Tom F. Driver, a teacher and historian of the theatre as well as a critic, who claims that the issues in the play are "sensationally overdrawn and the characters too neatly divided into the good and the bad."[2] Driver, measuring against the works of Beckett and Ionesco, finds Miller's plays intellectually limited and his style anachronistic. While Driver in 1970 could, and did, use a John Gassner 1954 essay as authority and support for his own position, by 1960 Gassner had changed his mind and recognized that the play would live long after its political implications had been forgotten; Gassner concludes his later study of *The Crucible* by calling it a powerful drama that surpasses others both in America and abroad.[3]

There is, to be obvious about it, a world of difference between New York theater reviewers and critics and the academic critic-scholar. The time frame, purpose, depth of investigation, training, and techniques are very different for each. The most significant research, as well as the greatest depth of perceptivity and richness of insight into the play, have come from scholars associated with colleges and universities. The major Miller academic critic-scholars—Gerald Weales, John H. Ferres, C. W. E. Bigsby, Robert A. Martin, Thomas E. Porter, Robert W. Corrigan, Leonard Moss, and Benjamin Nelson (author of what is still the most readable book on Miller—with the exception of *Timebends*)—all begin with the assumption that *The Crucible* is important and worthy of serious scholarly investigation. As Weales has concluded, "anyone with a touch of conscience, a hint of political interest, a whisper of moral concern will be drawn to *The Crucible*."[4]

Yet, it may be the students of these scholars, those students who are now reading and rereading the play, who will be the final arbiters. If literary history teaches anything at all, it is that authoritative estimations sometimes are—as Miller himself might say—whimsical at best, fraudulent at worst. As Miller did, in fact, say, "one approaches writers from one's own historical moment" (*Timebends*, 228). The play's reputation rests with generations of college students who, as the politics of the world readjust, are now interested in witchcraft, American history, and the politics of the past in this nation. As they go forward, establishing their own literary evaluations, critical reception, as well as codes of conduct, moral and ethical values, and knowledge of themselves, they might be well served by a recognition of the work of those who came before—and by remembering the words of Sheridan Morley in his review of the National Theatre's 1990 revival of the play in London: "*The Crucible* has never in purely dramatic terms been Miller's best play, but it is perhaps his greatest attempt and claim to be the keeper of the American historical conscience in this century, and that alone explains the need for constant revival."[5]

A READING

"You call this sport?" Parris (Noble Shropshire) and Abigail (Justine Bateman), act 1.

Photo by Martha Swope. Reproduced by permission of Gene Feist and the Roundabout Theatre Company.

4

"In the Closet or on the Stage?":
The Reader and an Audience

"Is the accuser always holy now? Were they born this morning as clean as God's fingers?"

—Proctor

A play is most often written by one person, but the theater is by nature a communal art form. Miller is well aware that his plays will be subject in performance to the talents and interpretations of actors, directors, light and set designers, and so forth, but he is experienced enough as a writer to know that he has direct access—as a writer of an essay, fiction, or poetry might—to his reader only through the published play. Thus, *The Crucible* must be made to work for the reader as closet drama as well as for an audience in public performance.

It is a given in the theatrical world that it is much better to see a play produced in a theater and to share the experience with the other members of an audience; Miller himself acknowledges that the theatrical experience is educational and inspirational in the most fundamental way. It is in the theater, Miller insists, that a sense of human relatedness allows for the formation of judgments as to what is funny and the appropriate emotional responses to a work. The common experience in the theater, Miller believes, thus enhances a sense of community in people. It refreshes the spirit to be able to share both the reactions of other people in the audience and the experiences of characters on the stage.

As an aware and actively participating member of the theatrical profession, Miller knows very well what other professionals can bring to the presentation of drama. He was, for instance, very appreciative of Elia Kazan's direction of *All My Sons* and *Death of a Salesman,* and as rehearsals progressed on *The Crucible,* Miller perceived what he took to be misconceptions and misdirections on the part of the play's director, Jed Harris. On the other hand, Miller was cognizant of the importance of Jo Mielziner's setting and light designs for *Death of a Salesman.* He also recognized the importance of the set design of Boris Aronson and the costumes of Edith Lutyens to the overall effect of *The Crucible.* Nevertheless, when business began to fall off in the summer months of 1953 during *The Crucible*'s initial run, Miller himself redirected the play, removing the sets to save the costs of stagehands and playing it in black with white lights that never moved from beginning to end. He found the play stronger for the new simplicity in production values.

Theatrical effects and the experience of attending a performance are, of course, unavailable to many readers of the play. To compensate for that, Miller provides editions of the published play with a detailed set of stage directions. Moreover, his direct comments in the text are almost as elaborate as the infamous prefaces that accompany George Bernard Shaw's plays. Miller makes substantive elaborations on the historical data and his use of them, describes most characters in relation to their historical models, and provides a thoughtful explanation of his method. In sum, he shares with his readers his own explication of the text, often in light of his original intentions.

The published text also provides a note on the historical accuracy of the play and appends "Echoes down the Corridor," a brief description of the final resolution and disposition (as accurately as it can be known beyond the misty avenues of legend) of those who survived the events of 1692.

Miller restaged *The Crucible* in July 1953 with a new cast and an additional scene (of which, more later), to satisfy his own sense of the proper presentation of the play. He felt that the play's original director, Jed Harris, had been mistaken in conceiving of the play's production as some sort of "Dutch painting," a classical play that had to be nobly performed (*Timebends,* 344). The dramatist believed that while *The Crucible* had succeeded as a play, it had failed commercially because the original production had cooled down what he meant to be a hot play that explored, among other themes, the guilt of illicit sexuality.

Always one to be deeply involved in the production of his plays, increasingly in recent years Miller has come to direct his own plays. His dual relationship to the material, as both writer and director, nicely parallels the ideal for his audience—to experience the drama both on the page and on the stage, to read, then see the play. Being informed by the dramatist's careful gloss on *The Crucible,* while in many ways essential to a deeper appreciation of it, is no substitute for the nuances added by the performance of Arthur Kennedy or George C. Scott as Proctor, or Colleen Dewhurst as Elizabeth, or Justine Bateman, who played Abigail Williams almost at the edge of rage in the 1990 Roundabout Theatre's revival. A careful reading of the play, perhaps augmented by available scholarly perceptions of it, along with the suggestive details of performance creates an ideal circumstance. When witnessing a production of the play may not be feasible or practical, however, a reader can illuminate the corners of his or her closet by attention to the matters of setting, structure, theme, and character.

"Why—? Why do you come, yellow bird?" Abigail (Justine Bateman) and cast, act 3.

Photo by Martha Swope. Reproduced by permission of Gene Feist and the Roundabout Theatre Company.

5

Mise-en-scène

"Why—? Why do you come, yellow bird?"

—Abigail

SETTING

The stage setting and use of physical properties have become increasingly important in the modern theater, more so than in Greek or Elizabethan drama, say, and the knowledgeable and experienced playwright is well aware of how each may serve his purposes. As such, Miller chose to reverse the trend and to simplify the demands upon stagecraft for this play. The sets, set dressing, and decor for *The Crucible* are quite simple when compared to the settings for other typical dramas of the 1950s. The sets and sparse furnishings for the four different locales are basically uncomplicated and easily rearranged to suit the specific needs of each act.

Act 1 is played entirely in a small upstairs bedroom in the home of Reverend Samuel Parris. A bed, a chest, a chair, a small table, and a candle are the only furnishings. This setting provides the dramatist with two elements that are requisite to his cause. First, he wants an "air of clean spareness" (3) that suits his audience's expectations as to verisimilitude: this is, after all, meant to represent Salem in 1692. More important to his purpose, all is to appear like wood, and the colors are "raw and unmellowed" (3). It is this sense of woodenness, with its suggestion of inflexibility and stiffness, that establishes the character of a province that appeared to the European world of the time as "a barbaric frontier inhabited by a set of fanatics" (4).

The wooden and expressionless feeling carries over to Proctor's house, the setting for act 2, but this time the setting is humanized by the presence of a cupboard, eating utensils, and a fireplace. Act 3 takes place in the vestry room of the Salem meetinghouse, which here serves as the anteroom of the general court. Its two high windows, heavy beams, plain bench, long meeting table, and walls bare of adornment are perfect to make the room appear "solemn, even forbidding" (83).

The final setting, in act 4, is a cell in Salem jail, again served by a wooden quality, this time to enhance an air of unnaturalness and lifelessness. The only furnishings beneath a high window, this time barred, are two wooden benches. Here, as in the rest of the play, the setting not only matches the historical models, but also establishes the proper mood and tone; in its very woodenness, it provides a commentary on the society and culture of 1692 Salem.

Furthermore, the original Broadway production and most recent revivals are enriched by a set in which "the roof rafters are exposed" (3). This detail reinforces the sense of being indoors. The second scene of act 2 (148–52), which Miller added, then deleted, may not have fit comfortably into the play because it is the only scene that would be set outdoors, in the wild. Whatever the scene might have added, it violates the sense of confinement and restriction represented by the bare wood of the other sets, as well as the limitations imposed by the exposed roof rafters. It is not just the cell in the jail of act 4 that shows confinement: the feeling is equally important for act 2, in Proctor's home, the setting for Proctor and Elizabeth's discussion about the nature and quality of their marriage.

Yet, as much as these particular sets enrich the play, physical setting may not be crucial for *The Crucible*. For Miller's own restaging of the play in July 1953, the set design consisted entirely of black drapes. The success of this and other simple productions of the play testifies to the power of its drama and its universal appeal. The point is not that *The Crucible* can be played economically and with little fuss, but that it plays—whether enhanced by a setting or in the simplest set. The simplicity of setting complements the complexity of the play's matter.

PROPS

The handling and management of stage properties is one of the theater's thankless but crucial tasks. The minute attention to detail of a property mistress, property master, or stage manager is seldom appreciated until something is *not* where it is supposed to be during performance. If a reader or member of the audience, however, does not note the significance of the prop's use, it is tantamount to its not being there.

The list of stage properties for *The Crucible* is, like the set, comparatively simple. Not all want discussion. Some, however, are significant in themselves or to stage business that advances the story or reveals something of character.

There are minor elements that suggest small aspects of time or character. These would include John Proctor's rifle (49; 62), the cider he drinks (51), and the whip he uses to intimidate Mary Warren (59), all in act 2. In the deleted two-point scene between Abigail and Proctor at night, he carries a lantern, which serves to represent and illuminate his "seeing her madness" (149). Of the same order is Rebecca Nurse's walking stick, which suggests age and infirmity on her initial entrance and serves to contrast her with Giles Corey, who enters immediately after her. Though eleven years her senior, Giles needs no cane, for he "is knotted with muscle, canny, inquisitive, and still powerful" (25).

This initial contrast will be significant as the two meet their different fates in the play's conclusion. There, Rebecca, weak from hunger and bereft of her walking stick, almost collapses. Her presence, along with the story of Giles Corey's power and fortitude, will serve as admonishment and inspiration for Proctor.

Props of a different sort, some obvious, others not so readily apparent, serve the play in more significant ways. The first of these are the half dozen heavy books the Reverend John Hale is loaded down with on his initial entrance. They establish him at the play's outset as the intellectual, the scholarly minister. When Parris, a Harvard College graduate who is—as Corey comically will point out—better instructed "in arithmetic" (29) than in ministry, observes how heavy the books are, Hale replies, "they must be; they are weighted with authority" (36). This remark underscores his own authoritative personality. It is further significant that Hale, one of the play's dynamic characters— dynamic in the sense that he grows significantly across the time the play's action spans—is *without* his books as he ministers in a real way to the condemned and "goes among them that will hang" (123) in the final act. The evaporation of Hale's books between acts 1 and 4 marks not only the transformation in his character, but a change in the role of the clergy from the seventeenth-century's scholar-minister to a ministry of another, more humane sort, as the power of the theocracy begins to wane.

Two significant stage properties serve to explicate and propel the plot in act 2. The use of the poppet (56; 74–75) and needle by which Abigail dupes Mary Warren into entrapping Elizabeth and indicating to the authorities her implication in witchcraft is not especially subtle, either in the deed or as a theatrical device. More elusive than the small rag doll is the pot of rabbit stew in the fireplace which provides the opening business for act 2 and a point of discussion for academic critics.[1] Momentarily alone in the common room of his house, Proctor swings the pot out of the fire and tastes the stew. Not pleased, he seasons it with salt and quickly returns the pot into the fireplace as he hears Elizabeth descending the stairs. Shortly thereafter, he compliments her on how well seasoned the stew is. She blushes with pleasure and says, "I took great care" (50). This salting of the stew does not constitute a serious deception in an intimate domestic moment where the unstated agenda is, after all, his previous adultery, but it is important enough for an audience or reader to note. It is a mildly humorous event in a play that does not have much funny about it; moreover, it is a conciliatory gesture by a husband to a wife who is feeling estranged. Proctor here means to please Elizabeth even in the littlest things. In human terms, it is exactly the sort of gesture a marriage partner might make to palliate a transgression or attempt to ameliorate a lingeringly uncomfortable atmosphere.

Two other props, the warrant for Elizabeth's arrest and her husband's confession, serve to demonstrate Proctor's growth while also providing a nice balance for the play. At the end of act 2, just before the halfway mark of the play, Proctor tears up the warrant in a rage (76). The piece of paper and Proctor's action match, balance, and prefigure his action in the play's penultimate moment, when he tears up his own signed confession, which might have let him live. In a rage when he tears up the warrant, he is "weeping in fury" (144) as he later tears and crumples the confession. An examination of these balancing points reveals that, for all his rage and fury, it is not the same Proctor who acts in each instance. When he tears up the warrant, he does so to protect his wife; there is, in the final action, something larger at stake. It has been disclosed that his wife will live because she is pregnant. The destruction of the confession means that there is something different and more important at risk than his life—his name.

A brief comment may be in order on one "prop" that does *not* appear in the play and is significant precisely because of its absence—the "yellow bird" (114–15). The fact that the audience, like Proctor, does not see the yellow bird that the girls claim to see indicates Abigail's cunning and her ability to manipulate the other girls and induce mass hysteria. It is a powerfully theatrical scene, yet it reassures the audience that they, like Proctor, possess common sense, and that there are rational explanations for the occurrences in the court and throughout Salem. Abigail points up toward the exposed roof rafters, but the audience follows Proctor's indicting finger to Abby, who has gulled the court.

SETTING AS METAPHOR

The settings of the individual acts and the order of their arrangement may be suggestive. The first two acts are set in private homes and an audience is offered parallels and differences between the two. In both houses, there is hope that the private matters within may come to an intramural resolution. On the other hand, the final two acts are set in public places, because the things that began as private affairs have burned like fires into their public venues.

Act 1 is set in a room in Parris's house in which the only access for light is a narrow window. Parris is "a widower with no interest in children, or talent with them" (3), and the house he keeps with his slave Tituba for his niece Abigail and his 10-year-old daughter Betty reflects his personality. There is no evidence of a woman or any affection about this house. More than merely spare, it is seems sterile.

In act 2, while Proctor's living room looks much like the room in Parris's house, the small differences suggest the presence of a couple, a man and a woman living there. A door opens on the fields outside. While the audience never sees them, the Proctors have three sons, the source of warm inquiry and affectionate conversation. There is in this home a sense of fecundity, of the farm and flowers, even if, for the moment, it is being thwarted.

Act 3, set in the most public of places, will bring forth the most secret, most private revelations. If the room is meant to be forbidding, there is hopeful sunlight pouring through the two high windows as the act opens. There is no such hope in act 4's Salem jail, which is set "in darkness" (121), the darkness deepest before the final dawn on the morning of execution.

In the first act, the audience is privy to the activities within the privacy of the home of a public man, Samuel Parris, a minister. In the second act, the audience penetrates the invisible fourth wall into the privacy of a private man, Proctor; yet, as in act 1, the activity within this home turns public. The third act portrays the engagement of the private man with a powerful and forceful public man, Deputy Governor Danforth, in a public display of what had been the private man's introspective and secret dilemma. Act 4 witnesses both public display and intimate moments between man and wife in a public place and the growth of the private man into a hero.

Abigail Williams, the driving force for what happens in all four stage settings, is seen once in a private place in act 1 and once in public in act 3, then escapes all, including responsibility, judgment, and association with any specific setting. The mise-en-scène, however, is only the "place" where the playwright begins; he must then consider shape, form, and movement, all in relation to structure.

6

Structure

"She has an arrow in you yet, John Proctor, and you know it well!"

BY ACT

To begin before the beginning, it is a common feature of good dramatic structure that the tale being told starts in the middle. Under no circumstances should it begin at the beginning. This applies to Shakespeare and Sophocles as well as Arthur Miller. To cite two brief and readily accessible illustrations, Hamlet's father has been killed before the play opens, and Oedipus has already killed Laius and married Jocasta before his play opens. Likewise, *The Crucible* begins in medias res. Two events crucial to the drama have already taken place before the curtain rises—the dancing in the woods by the girls and Parris's discovery of it, and, more important, Proctor's sexual relationship with Abigail.

Nor is this the only characteristic that marks *The Crucible* as a well-made play. A well-made play ordinarily, but not always, follows a particular pattern: exposition, rising action, climax, falling action (or denouement), and catastrophe. This structure applies to Miller's play in the following way: act 1 provides necessary exposition; acts 2 and 3 consist of rising action, culminating in the climax in the final moments of act 3; act 4 is clearly denouement, and the catastrophe occurs in the play's final lines. The rising action is set in motion by what is called the exciting force—in this case, it is Abigail Williams.

BY SCENES

This structural analysis might be further refined to examine the care that has gone into the play's anatomy on a scene-by-scene basis. While the individual moments are not marked as scenes in the text, they clearly constitute such. In musical terms they might be characterized as trio, duet, quartet, ensemble, and so forth. The play opens with a tableau of Parris kneeling beside the bed of his daughter Betty, which quickly evolves into a scene with Parris, Tituba, and Abigail that provides opening exposition. This scene (3–12) runs until the entrance of the Putnams and contains a significant line of demarcation when Abigail explains what happened in the forest. She here speaks the truth: "It were sport, uncle!" (11). Up to this point it is still not too late to stop things and turn back the course of events, but Parris's character weaknesses and the grievances of the Putnams, real and imagined, exacerbate the situation. The scene that includes the Putnams (13–17) provides more exposition, but this early on some members of the audience may begin to believe that there are too many characters, especially for a small upper bedroom. The next scene (18–20), with Mary Warren, Abby, and the dissembling Betty provides crucial exposition and prepares the audience for the entrance of John Proctor (20). The two-point scene between Proctor and Abigail provides additional exposition, but, more significant, it is here that the rising action of the play begins. Proctor's relationship with Abigail is clarified, and his resolve to end the sexual liaison moves Abby to her next level of attack. Although it will not seem to be a concerted plan of action,

Abby, an opportunist, will seize whatever presents itself at the moment—much like Shakespeare's master villain Iago—the pivotal character (as Abigail is here) in the play in which he appears.

Following Proctor's rejection of her advances and sensual familiarity, the smarting Abby is silent for 17 pages, until she is drawn into matters by Hale. During this time, Rebecca Nurse, Giles Corey, and the Putnams provide further exposition, but Abigail is the presence of greatest importance. Questioned by Hale (42), Abby now ups the ante and the stakes get higher. She uses Tituba as a scapegoat, but more significant is her final outburst (48), which sets Betty rising from her bed. Her action has been fed not merely by an attempt to escape censure, but by a desperation inspired, not by witches or the devil, but by Proctor's rejection of her.

While Abby does not appear in act 2, which is set eight days later in Proctor's house, or in act 4, she remains the pivotal character. She is the engine of the play who by her actions creates conflict and drives the play forward. Act 2 opens with Elizabeth, a new character to the play's action (it is not uncommon for playwrights to introduce a new and significant character at the opening of a second act to perk an audience's interest), in a lengthy two-point scene with John (49–55) that provides more exposition and development of character. The subsequent scene (55–60) with Mary Warren, the Proctors, and the poppet accelerates the rising action and leads to a second significant two-point scene between Proctor and Elizabeth (60–62), and the pace of the play quickens perceptibly. The level of tension in this two-point scene has also clearly risen; the action rises to a pitch clearly well above that of the opening scene of the act. Innuendo and a rhetorical care not to be excessively hurtful have been replaced by accusations and confrontation. Elizabeth knows that the sexual attraction between Proctor and Abigail is still there, and baldly says, "she has an arrow in you yet, John Proctor, and you know it well!" (62). Elizabeth knows Abby wants her dead, and John, as well, "knows it is true" (61).

At this point, Hale enters and the three-point scene that follows establishes Proctor's integrity. He will "not conceal" (65) his dislike and distrust of Parris, nor the reasons for it. Proctor is a good man who has put the roof and hung the door on the church (66), who objects to the materialism of Parris (65), and who demonstrates himself to be a man of common sense as far as witches and witchcraft are concerned (69). There is obvious dramatic irony in John's inability to remember "adultery" when Hale quizzes him on the commandments—and even more poignant, wry irony that Elizabeth must be the one to remind him (67).

In the act's fifth scene, Giles Corey and Francis Nurse bring news of their wives (70–71), and the rise in action becomes steep. The scene serves as a reminder of the economic base of the "crying out" that was suggested in act 1. Ezekiel Cheever and Marshal Herrick enter with the warrant, the needle in the poppet is disclosed, and the act rushes toward its conclusion. Miller provides Proctor with what will become a celebrated line, often believed to be pointed at McCarthyism and the witch-hunt of the 1950s: "Is the accuser always holy now?" (77). Hale counsels Proctor to think "what may have drawn from heaven such thundering wrath upon you all" (79), and Proctor is "reached by Hale's words" (79), not for any matters of witchcraft but for the guilt he bears for his secret, the sexual "sin" with Abigail. The act ends with Proctor resolved to expose Abby's intentions. This act has progressed from a quiet domestic scene of a man and wife having supper to the point where the action of the play can no longer be confined within the privacy of homes but explodes along with Proctor into the public realm.

Act 3 is set in the vestry of the Salem meetinghouse, which is being used as the anteroom of the general court, signifying that the play has moved from homes and personal affairs to the arena of the court and broad social matters. The act begins with Corey's reminder to the audience of the economic base that has added fuel to the fires—"Thomas Putnam is reaching out for land" (84)—and Miller does not miss an opportunity to indicate that something is upside down in a search for justice in which "one calls up witnesses to prove his innocence" (100).

The major impetus to the rising action here, as in act 2, is the introduction of a new character. Once again, it is more than just a structural nicety of good theater, for the addition this time is a forceful and powerful character, Deputy Governor Danforth. It has been

quite succinctly pointed out that in drama the presence of two determined, uncompromising forces in combat will "create a virile rising
conflict."[1] Danforth and Proctor are the two determined, uncompromising forces in conflict here, but, while it makes for exciting drama to
watch the two men—and listen to them—Proctor's greatest conflict
will not be with Danforth here in act 3, but with himself in the play's
final scene. But by this point in the drama, Proctor has already begun
his growth. He is no longer fighting just to save his wife's life, for it has
been disclosed that Elizabeth is safe for the present because of her
pregnancy. As Danforth recognizes, Proctor's "purpose is somewhat
larger" (92), but it is not, as Danforth suspects, any attempt to subvert
the court or undermine the authority of the judges. Elizabeth lies in an
attempt to save her husband's name (113), and events rush to a pre-
cipitous level.

There are three tremendous moments in act 3, each of which
might have served as a climax to the play. The mass hysteria as Abigail
shivers visibly and feels "a wind" leads to hysteria in the other girls
and, ultimately, to Proctor's confession of adultery (110). But this is
topped by Abigail's theatrically chilling "yellow bird" (114) and her
moment of triumph as Mary Warren rushes to Abigail, who "out of
her infinite charity, reaches out and draws the sobbing Mary to her"
(119). All of this is part of an extended climax, but the exact climactic
moment is Proctor's explosive speech to Danforth, which ends the act:
"A fire, a fire is burning! I hear the boot of Lucifer, I see his filthy face!
And it is my face, and yours, Danforth! For them that quail to bring
men out of ignorance, as I have quailed, and you quail now when you
know in all your black hearts that this be fraud—God damns our kind
especially, and we will burn, we will burn together!" (120).

Three months pass between the moment of this speech and the
opening of act 4, which is almost the perfect denouement. After the
tripartite explosions that provide the play's climax at the conclusion of
act 3, this final act seems almost reconciled and peaceful, though it will
build again to John Proctor's decisions at the play's finish.

Miller spends part of the act tidying up. The conversation among
Parris, Danforth, and Hathorne about the events in Andover,
Massachusetts, which "will have no part of witchcraft" (127), indicates

that times are changing; as the seventeenth century draws to a close, people will begin to become enlightened. This moment projects the theater audience into the ultimate resolution, beyond the final actions of Miller's play: the audience is reminded that the power of the theocracy will be broken.

Another loose end is tied up with the final disposition of Abigail Williams. She and Mercy Lewis have fled with six months of Parris's salary, stolen from his strongbox (126). With Abby gone, the conclusion of the play and its final impact will belong penultimately to Proctor and Elizabeth and finally to Proctor alone.

In a final two-point scene, Elizabeth confesses to some culpability in her husband's infidelity, but ironically it is she who brings him the news of Giles Corey's death (135), which will form a part of Proctor's final decision to accept his own fate. The danger in a play so loaded with histrionics and theatrical pyrotechnics as Betty's rising from her bed and the scene of mass hysteria in act 3 is that audiences will overlook the quiet beauty and significant drama of the smaller moments between John and Elizabeth, the two scenes in act 2 and this final one. Perhaps Clifford Odets observed better than he knew. The play *is,* in part, about a marriage. The final temptation, however, will be Proctor's alone. In the final scene (142–45), Proctor wants to live; his rejection of the opportunity to do so provides the substance of one of this drama's major themes, and the offstage drumroll announces the catastrophe.

EXITS AND ENTRANCES

Those places where characters enter and exit are a part of a play's dramatic structure. When a character comes in or goes out, "he must do so of necessity. His action must help the development of the conflict and be part of the character in the process of revealing himself" (Egri, 252). The first entrances of Elizabeth and Danforth, as has been suggested, come at precisely the right moments; the audience meets new, interesting people at the proper dramatic time.

One entrance, however, deserves special attention, one that does help the development of the conflict and is, indeed, part of the character in the process of revealing himself: the entrance of John Proctor into the play. What is Proctor doing in a small upper bedroom in Parris's home? If it seems that there are a goodly number of people in that upper bedroom in act 1, and we wonder what they are doing coming and going, other than being characters in a play, the one thing we ought not wonder about is what has brought Proctor to that upper chamber. The excuse he provides, that he has come to see what "mischief your uncle's brewin' now" (22), is just not likely. He has come to see Abby. In this first exchange between them in the play (20–24), note not just Abigail's reactions and comments to Proctor, but the "suggestion of a knowing smile on his face" (21); as she draws closer to him, note "his smile widening" (22). He still does look up at her window as he passes, he does think of her "softly from time to time" (23), and although he says his resolve is firm and he is trying, he is "angered—at himself as well" as her (23), for Proctor is still attracted to Abby. He denies it here, yet Abby knows it, Elizabeth reinforces it in act 2, and Proctor finally concedes that he "thought of her softly" (110) as late in the play as his confession to Danforth and the general court.

THE EFFECT OF THE "BRIEF NEW SCENE"

The final element of structure to be considered is the missing, added, and, once again, deleted scene. Act 2, scene 2 (148–52) was added when Miller redirected and recast the play during the summer of 1953, in the middle of its original Broadway run. It has been deleted ever since in almost all professional productions. It must be said, in candor, that the play does not need to be any longer than it is as it stands. Yet this additional scene is quite brief. At the time of its addition, moreover, Brooks Atkinson, for one, liked it very much. He observed that the changes improved the play, adding heart and human warmth, and he concluded that the "brief new scene between Abigail

Williams and John Proctor . . . completely motivates their clash in the following scene laid in the courtroom."[2]

The eliminated two-point scene is set in the woods late at night. Proctor has come in an attempt to dissuade Abby from her role in the burgeoning witch-hunt; she, in a nightgown with her hair down, is caught up both in her original desire to be Proctor's wife and in a new madness inspired by the rampant hysteria. Miller added the scene to revive a power and passion he felt the original production lacked, having cooled off what he intended to be a very hot play. He then deleted the scene because it distracted from the play's inner theme of conscience and a "name."

There is a gain to be had by adding this scene. Abby, who has been established as a principal character in act 1, is absent for all of act 2 and she will not appear at all in act 4. This scene allows the playwright to bring a strong central character back after a long spell offstage in the green room. On the other hand, there are quite good reasons for deleting the scene. On the most superficial level, it is not practical for Abby to be in act 2 or act 4. She has been thrown out of Proctor's house and barred by Elizabeth from what is the setting for the entire second act, and she is gone from the play by the time of the jail scene.

Moreover, the deleted scene between Proctor and Abigail itself violates the play's sense of circumscription. All the other action of the play is confined indoors, and this sense of confinement is thematically central—both in the story of the fall of theocratic power and its analogue in McCarthyism.

Finally, Abby appears quite mad in the deleted scene. She is so apparently caught up in the witchcraft that she has had her head turned—but that is inconsistent with the Abby of act 1, who tells Proctor that Betty is only frightened and "gone silly somehow" (21) because Parris "leaped in on us" (22) as they were dancing in the woods; it is even more inconsistent with the cunning and manipulative Abby of act 3, Abigail the opportunist.

Why not more of Abby? Why is Abby off for two acts? Why does Miller allow so hot a possibility to cool off? While Abigail is the central character, she is not the protagonist. She functions as the pivotal character much as Iago does in Shakespeare's *Othello;* not that the pair are necessarily alike or of equal quality as dramatic entities, but they are similar in dramatic function. Arthur Miller had to be very careful with a character who is this strong. If Miller were to utilize more of Abigail, the play might seem to be *about* Abigail, or it might even seem to be a story of John and Abigail. It is neither of these; it is a play about the protagonist Proctor.

7

Themes and Conflict

A fire, a fire is burning! I hear the boot of Lucifer, I see his filthy face!
And it is my face, and yours, Danforth! For them that quail to bring
men out of ignorance.

—Proctor

There is a curious dichotomy to dramatic characters. In conflict they
are forced to reveal themselves, and this self-revelation is an important
part of an audience's interest in and attraction to the play. It is through
conflicts between characters that themes develop. A playwright who
sets out to write about certain themes usually has a poor approach to
the creation of drama: he or she is most likely to end up with polemic,
a work that is preachy or too didactic.

Thanks to Miller's skillful development of characters, the themes
of *The Crucible* are successfully presented. Sheridan Morley is representative of critics when he says that the play is "a company piece
about honor and betrayal, integrity and compromise, state and church,
home and prison" (Morley, 64–65). Since character, conflict, and
theme are intimately related, what are the basic and elementary conflicts through which these themes are revealed?

Ordinarily, the conflict in a work of literature may be one of several kinds: man versus nature, man versus man, man versus society, or man versus himself. *The Crucible* ignores almost entirely the struggle with the forces of nature. The only concession to it is the almost unnoticed detail that in act 2 Proctor does not venture forth from his home without his rifle. Despite this tiny nod in the direction of the state of the wilderness around Salem at the end of the seventeenth century, Proctor is, for the most part, almost a poet in his relation to the elements of nature, with an Emersonian or Whitmanesque love of the earth, his farm, and its flowers (51).

More to the point is the second of the classic conflicts, the struggle of the protagonist with another person, and here Miller provides a fecund field. Proctor's struggles with other people are figured in what are essentially minor conflicts with Parris, Hale, and even Giles Corey. His major conflicts in this arena are with Abigail and Elizabeth.

The most obvious conflict in the drama is the struggle of the protagonist Proctor against society—a force personified by Thomas Putnam, Judge Hathorne, and especially Deputy Governor Danforth. The most profound conflict in the play, however, is the most subtle; the battle for ascendancy of the elements within Proctor himself. It is the resolution of this conflict that will provide the play's conclusion and its lasting merit and meaning.

On its most overt level, *The Crucible* is a play about the collapse of the power of theocracy in Massachusetts and on this continent. It expresses, moreover, the will to stand up to authoritarian inquisition and those who are absolute in their convictions. Miller says that he knows there is nothing as visionary "and as blinding as moral indignation." He confesses that it is only possible to hear, and understand, the voices of those hanging judges "if one had known oneself the thrill of having been absolutely right" (*Timebends,* 115). Where does the play actually, as Miller claims, send the audience's—especially young people's—minds in relation to liberty, in relation to the rights of people? What has *The Crucible* to do with liberty and the rights of people? The play's most obvious, and to Miller, most important theme is "its message of resistance to a tyranny" (*Timebends,* 348).

There are other themes implicit in the play. *The Crucible* examines the phenomenon of hysteria and the effects of hysteria. The scenes that conclude acts 1 and 3 (48; 114–19) illustrate the effectiveness of this hysteria and how it can spread. Miller emphasizes the suggestibility of hysterics; the implications for an indictment of McCarthyism are readily apparent. Once a nation began to see Communists in the state department, in the army, in the arts, it was hard not to see them or fellow travelers everywhere. Further critiquing the hysteria of accusation, the play looks briefly at revenge as a motive for human action. For example, Putnam, still nursing a grudge because of the rejection of his wife's brother-in-law for the position as minister of Salem and the appointment of Parris in his stead, is "the guiding hand behind the outcry" (26).

One of the principal thematic elements explored by this play is the power of guilt, especially sexual guilt, but this matter is so important to the kelson, the central structure, of the play that it will be discussed more fully in a separate chapter. Two additional thematic concerns are closely related—fear and the power of ignorance. The play focuses upon the power of ignorance—both the tendency toward superstition and slavish devotion to what people perceive to be "religious" principles.

Ignorance, in general, is the medium in which fear grows. The play explores two kinds of fear—first, the fear many ordinary citizens have of engaging or questioning the social apparatuses that are, in theory, designed to protect them, here specifically the court and a judicial system. Hale makes this plain when he says, "there is a prodigious fear of this court in the country" (98). Fear is related to the power of ignorance, of course, but there is, the play suggests, a worse kind of fear. In Proctor's exceptional speech at the end of act 3, he says that he and Danforth are especially damned. Why? Because Proctor and Danforth know better. They are not ignorant men; they understand the reality of what is going on and, each for his own reasons, have hesitated to place a rein on the course of events. Both have "quailed"—that is, drawn back in fear and recoiled—from their human responsibility "to bring men out of ignorance" (120). For his own private reasons, and in his guilt concerning his relations with Abby, Proctor has hesitated to act. Danforth has done so because, as forceful, powerful, and knowledgeable as he is, he represents an office; he is an implement of the status quo, a representative of the theocracy who, knowing better, does not allow his humor and sophistication to "interfere with an exact loyalty to his position and his cause" (85). He is the law here.

This "law" and its relation to justice form an additional theme in the play. Arthur Miller has a devotion to civil liberty and justice—even when justice is at odds with the law. This sense of justice was much on his mind in the 1950s. Indeed, his next major play, *A View from the Bridge,* focuses on law and justice. It is no coincidence that several of his major characters—among them Alfieri, the narrator of *View,* and Quentin, in whose mind, thought, and memory the action of *After the Fall* takes place—are lawyers. Even if the judges in *The Crucible* are not lawyers in the sense the term is known today, Miller is endlessly fascinated by—and engages—those moments when the law and justice are at odds.

One of the reasons for injustice in *The Crucible* is that this legal system presumes guilt until innocence is proven. Danforth says, "in an ordinary crime, how does one defend the accused? One calls up witnesses to prove his innocence" (100). The situation is complicated by the fact that all of the evidence is not put forth (84), and is exacerbated because the accuser is "always holy now" (77). The sense that a person is seen as guilty until proven innocent may not stain someone forever, but the stigma lasts longer than might be imagined. In fact, the historical John Procter's letter of 23 July 1692 to five members of the Boston clergy, on behalf of himself and his fellow prisoners, points out that the community had "Condemned us already before our Tryals" (Burr, 362). While this "guilty until proven innocent" is part and parcel of what constitutes a witch-hunt, it may be that Miller touches a deeper wellspring of human nature, the propensity that once one is accused, some people continue thereafter to suspect the worst. Perhaps this disposition to believe the worst of a man or woman accused of straying—or even rumored to have strayed—from accepted community norms or mores, is part of human nature; it thus carries the play beyond Salem and its McCarthy parallels to a universal ground.

What Henry James said of the development of his novels and short stories, that character must come before any idea of "plot" or setting and to do otherwise would be putting the cart before the horse, applies as well to drama and the fiction of others. The greatest writers do not merely write ideas; they write of people, encouraging readers to infer the ideas. This is not to suggest that writers must be without beliefs, convictions, and a central purpose, but that a writer, no matter what his or her propensity, political bias, or intention, cannot make speeches without compromising his or her work. The best works of the best writers, whether Henry James or Arthur Miller, demonstrate that. All of the themes and central ideas extrapolated from *The Crucible*'s conflicts are dependent upon character. It is character that is the sine qua non, the essential condition, the absolute prerequisite, to the creation of vibrant drama—and, to a certain extent, the secret to its enduring success.

8

Characters

I do think I see some shred of goodness in John Proctor. Not enough
to weave a banner with, but white enough to keep it from such dogs.
                                                                —Proctor

Since character creates plot, not vice versa, Miller's attention to character, and the audience's, are consequential matters. Critics have had
two major complaints about the characters in *The Crucible:* first, that
there are too many of them; second, that they are all drawn either too
good or too bad. An important critic who held the initial case to be
true was John Gassner, who wrote, "if there are obvious weaknesses in
the play, they result mainly from the fact that Proctor and his wife are
swamped by such a multiplicity of secondary characters."[1] Concerning
the second matter, it was no less an intellectual luminary than Eric
Bentley who, in the *New Republic,* damned the play as melodrama
because the villains were too evil and the heroes too good.

　　As to Gassner's charges: are there too many characters in the
play? In act 1, the answer may seem to be yes. The setting is not, after
all, a public square on market day but a small bedroom in a minister's

residence. If the use of such a crowd seems to stretch a bit the audience's willingness to suspend their disbelief, there may be quite another way to evaluate the overall number of characters in the play. There are, in sum, 21 dramatis personae, and Miller as a social playwright and commentator needs the crowd to establish the pervasive ambience of neighborhood, of the village (using those terms in an anthropological sense). To understand Proctor and his actions, it is necessary to see them in the context of the characteristics, customs, and social relationships of his community. The dramatist wants that community visible onstage. That Miller feels strongly about this matter is demonstrated clearly in his comments about another of his plays, *A View from the Bridge,* and its protagonist, Eddie Carbone. The playwright much preferred the London production of that play—as he would the London production of *The Crucible*—because it was possible there to have at least 20 men and women surrounding the main action, while the practical economics of New York theater restricted the cast who were to represent the community to four actors.

Miller is quite capable of creating outstanding intimate drama on a smaller scale; *The Price,* after all, has a cast of only four. It is just that some of his principal protagonists, Proctor and Carbone among them, are best depicted on a broad and crowded canvas. What Miller has written of Carbone applies equally to Proctor. His mind "is not comprehensible apart from its relation to his neighborhood, his fellow workers, his social situation. His self-esteem depends upon their estimate of him, and his value is created largely by his fidelity to the code of his culture."[2] For "neighborhood" substitute "village," and for "workers" write "Puritans," and you have the situation of Proctor. Miller felt that *The Crucible,* written before *View,* was an important step toward a more self-aware drama because "the Puritan not only felt, but constantly referred his feelings to concepts, to codes and ideas of social and ethical importance" (*View,* vi–vii).

All of Miller's major protagonists—Willy Loman, Eddie Carbone, and John Proctor, to choose a few examples—are men who, if we are to understand them in any meaningful way, must be seen in the context of the communities in which they live. In another time or social environment, the actions of these men would take on an entirely different significance. In Miller's major plays, the community contains the ethos that the character is working with and against. It is the source of the moral energy in the play. Often, this community is visible, as it is in *The Crucible* and *A View from the Bridge*. (This accounts, in part, for a the greater success, to Miller's way of thinking, of those two plays in their London productions, where significantly lower costs allowed for larger casts than the pay scales of the New York theater would permit; in New York, it would be impossible to hire a crowd of on-stage witnesses to the play's action.) Even if it is not portrayed on the stage, as it is not in *Death of a Salesman,* the sense of community becomes a vital force for his principal protagonists. They are men (in Miller's major plays they are almost exclusively male) who must be seen in relation to the particular mores of the class of people to which they belong. The man is part of his society, and his society is an essential part of who he is. It is impossible to disentangle them.

Miller's protagonists begin by accepting their communities' values, living by their code—and then something goes wrong. This process may take years, as in *Death of a Salesman,* or it may happen very quickly, as in *A View from the Bridge* and *The Crucible.* Like Willy or Eddie Carbone, the hero may not be able to understand clearly what is happening; alternatively, like Proctor, he may know perfectly well where the source of the aberration lies.

Miller does not, however, belabor his characters' position in the social environment. He is a playwright, not a pollster, and he does not see his protagonists as sociological entities. To Miller, Eddie Carbone, Willy Loman, and John Proctor are dramatic characters, not real citizens. They do not have problems other than those with which he deals in his plays. The audience or reader can, of course, learn of the ambience of a particular culture in a fixed time and place by engaging his plays, but Miller is no local colorist. His genius transcends the specificity of a given milieu, or, more properly, fixes a time and place even as he transcends them.

Miller's credo is that "literature had to speak to the present condition of man's life and thus would implicitly have to stand against injustice as the destroyer of life" (*Timebends,* 596). Still the dramatist may best be seen as he sees himself—that is, as far less political than moral. For all his indictments of social, economic, and political problems, he is essentially a moralist, one who is concerned with ethics and enduring values.

As for Eric Bentley's reservation, a more carefully delineated and developed response is required. The term *character* needs to be parsed in relation to theatrical usage. The list of characters must be divided into major and minor, then subdivided into categories in which those characters who are static are separated from those who are dynamic, and then further refined as to degrees of culpability and the nature of each character's responsibilities in the unfolding events of the play.

Unlike all men under the Declaration of Independence, all dramatic characters are not created equal. They have varied theatrical functions and responsibilities, sometimes to the play's structure, and it would therefore be spurious to evaluate minor characters against the same measures as principal characters. There are low functionaries of the court, for instance, like Ezekiel Cheever, Marshal Herrick, and Hopkins. Much the same is true of Sarah Good and even Tituba. It is Parris's Barbados slave, of course, who will be used as a scapegoat by the crafty and quick-thinking Abigail to put off further questioning by Hale, but in borrowing her from history, the dramatist does not expect to develop her into a major character.

A careful look, however, at the episode that opens act 4 (121–23) suggests that the nearly drunk Herrick, Sarah Good, and Tituba provide more than the drunken gatekeeper scene borrowed from *Macbeth* that some critics take it to be. In fact, these minor characters are making fun of the concept of "the Devil" as real; the implication that they do not believe in demons or demonic possession any more than "a poor old cow with a hatful of milk" (123) adds an interesting tilt to the audience's understanding of the actual opinion of witchcraft held by much of the Salem community.

Likewise, a fresh look at the girls who fall under the sway of Abigail's influence is suggestive. Susanna Walcott and Mercy Lewis provide necessary exposition, and Betty Parris creates a moment of high drama for an act 1 curtain (48), but only Mary Warren is given a significant role to play. In act 2, Mary becomes arrogant and self-important as "an official of the court" (59) before she folds under the force of John Proctor's bullying. Her collapse anticipates and prefigures the way she will break again in act 3 under the influence of Abigail's will. Her reversal, which provides Abby's moment of triumph as she "reaches out and draws the sobbing Mary to her" (119), is prepared for and made credible by her wilting in her earlier confrontation with Proctor.

Taken together, Susanna, Mercy, Betty, and Mary form, in Miller's terms, "a klatch of repressed pubescent girls who, fearing punishment for their implicitly sexual revolt, began convincing themselves that they had been perverted by Satan" ("Again They Drink," 36). This sense of budding and repressed sexuality gives, in Freudian terms, a secondary meaning to the concern in act 1 about the girls' "flying."

Thus, of the 21 characters in the play, nine serve as less than consequential persons in their own right, and of the remaining dozen, half are fully realized, complex, complicated characters. As for remaining minor characters, one might just as well concede that Bentley may have a point. Rebecca Nurse is a model of goodness and Judge Hathorne is certainly unrelievedly evil, "a bitter, remorseless Salem judge" (85). Although Bentley is accurate, his observation would be significant only if the play were *about* Rebecca Nurse or Judge Hathorne. Even Rebecca's husband, Francis Nurse, is given dimension, and Giles Corey, who supplies small shards of comic relief in a play that otherwise has little, is hardly all good, but rather portrayed as a cantankerous and litigious old man. Rebecca Nurse and Giles Corey are much more important to the play because they represent pieces of a puzzle that Proctor must fit together in order to come to his final decision. More will be said in a later chapter concerning the implications of Proctor's willingness to hang.

The remaining minor characters, Ann Putnam and especially Thomas Putnam, deserve special attention. The fact that Mrs. Putnam has "laid seven babies unbaptized in the earth" (15) might ordinarily arouse audience sympathy, but her grief moves her to charge Rebecca Nurse with their "marvelous and supernatural murder" (71), so Mrs. Putnam becomes a party to the villainy. As has been pointed out earlier, Thomas Putnam is the sub-rosa architect for much of the substance of the witch-hunt. A vindictive, deeply embittered and resentful man who feels his own reputation has been sullied, Putnam bears much guilt for the continuation of the outcry. Ill will between Putnam and the Nurse family (26) and the dispute with Proctor over ownership of land (32) suggest that Corey is accurate when he roars to the court, "Thomas Putnam is reaching out for land" (84) and when he points out that "Putnam . . . is killing his neighbors for their land" (96). Although they are minor characters, the Putnams are hardly innocents in the madness that consumes Salem.

Also culpable is the Reverend Samuel Parris, but his liability to blame is of a different sort. While Putnam's part in the affair is active and pernicious, Parris's is passive—but no less a contributing factor. What Parris knows and withholds during the play's first scenes might have mitigated charges and had an ameliorating effect had he come forward sooner. His attempts to fan the flames of the ignited conflagration in the third act amount to little because everyone, including Danforth, has such small regard or respect for him. While both Parris and Putnam serve as antagonists to Proctor, they are not interchangeable villains. They are both overly concerned with material possessions, but Parris is an insecure, supercilious, vain, and paranoid individual about whom hangs a sense of confusion. If he displays an air of uncertainty about how to act in an effort to save face and his reputation, he, like the others that Miller indicts, also suffers from a sense of being absolutely right. If Parris is culpable, he is, nonetheless, a static rather than a dynamic character. If he seems somehow changed in the play's final act, the change is cosmetic, for all that has happened is that his fear—in the play's final scene, a fear of reprisal—has risen to the surface. Taken together, Parris, Putnam, Francis Nurse, and Corey as well represent the economic and social pressures Miller intends to show at work in the witch-hunt. To understand how anyone dare call these people witches—especially someone as highly respected as Rebecca Nurse—the audience must follow Miller's pointing finger and "look to the fields and boundaries of that time" (26). Long-standing bickering over boundaries and deeds, in the disguise of godliness, could be lifted from the dirt of the fields to "the arena of morality" (8).

Parris and Putnam are antagonists to Proctor, but neither is as interesting or as forceful in that role as Danforth. Proctor and the deputy governor recognize each other almost at once as worthy adversaries; they are equally determined and uncompromising forces—the hallmark of the conflict in superior drama. Proctor can laughingly draw old Giles Corey along (32), openly express his disdain for Parris (90), and stand up unequivocally to Putnam (30), but he senses a force of person in Danforth the equal of his own. For Danforth's part, the audience notes in production what a reader sees in the stage directions; the deputy governor continually "studies" Proctor by looking into his eyes (89, 90, 91) and Proctor "tries to meet his gaze" (91). Danforth is an experienced jurist with "thirty-two year at the bar" (100) whose judgments of people are often astute—"his contempt for Parris is clear" (101)—but he is seduced, "engaged and entered" (109) by Abigail's performance.

Yet Danforth is, like Proctor, intelligent and perceptive. He, like Proctor, is strong-willed and determined. His is a mind of equal rigor. He recognizes Proctor as a peer, but, unlike Proctor, he will not change. Danforth has humor, sophistication, and a strong personality, but he is not dynamic. He remains essentially single-minded and unchanged. Compare the Danforth of his entrance into the play in act 3 with the Danforth of his final appearance in act 4. He has been suspicious, he has had his doubts, he has been frightened, but because of his relationship with the court and the theocracy, he will not move. He shares culpability for the hangings at Salem, yet he remains a static character.

Of the three major dynamic characters in the play (the other two are Proctor and John Hale), perhaps the least understood is Elizabeth Proctor. She is, for the most part, a quiet person in a play filled with bombast and moments of high theatricality. She is a wronged wife who, like her husband, does not believe in witches (69), but who, despite an apparent insularity, is an astute judge of human character and relationships. Moreover, she grows significantly from the aggrieved homemaker of act 2, smarting from her husband's infidelity, to a woman who will, as she understands it, risk damnation of her immortal soul by lying to protect her husband's name. Beyond that, she will have developed to the point in act 4 when she confesses to a sense of some responsibility for her husband's transgression: "It needs a cold wife to prompt lechery" (137). She comes to know herself and her own motives even better: "I counted myself so plain, so poorly made, no honest love could come to me" (137). But her greatest advance is reaching the point, in the play's ultimate moment, when she can recognize and understand her husband's motivation as she allows him to go to his death: "He have his goodness now. God forbid I take it from him" (145).

The character in whom the dynamic change is most apparent is Reverend John Hale. He enters the play the complete intellectual, the scholarly minister burdened by his books. In the course of the play, he comes to recognize the falsity of the action unfolding before him. As he becomes a man of the enlightenment, there is a concomitant growth in his humanity. He, of all the play's characters, recognizes his part in the occurrences; his sense of his own guilt fathers his awareness, and he is repentant. More important, he acts upon his new knowledge. No longer the inquiring clergyman seeking spirits from another world, he allows his sharp intellectual faculties to be balanced by his heart, and he develops into a man who truly ministers as "he goes among them that will hang" (123).

If Abigail Williams is the play's pivotal character, she nevertheless cannot be termed dynamic. She is cunning, but she does not change. At the end of the play, she is the same as she was earlier. An incorrigible opportunist, she can shift the focus of attention from herself to Tituba and draw upon various things as they suit her purpose. The "yellow bird" that she talks to "in genuine conversation" (115) as she disrupts the procedures of the court at the end of act 3 has been planted in her consciousness, and in her bag of tricks, during Hale's attempt to question Betty in act 1: "perhaps some bird invisible to others comes to you—" (41). Moreover, she is stoic in what she will endure—including a needle "stuck two inches in the flesh of her belly" (74)—to achieve what she has resolved; replacing Elizabeth as Proctor's wife. And she is powerful enough not merely to stand up to, but to openly threaten, Danforth (108). This is, in addition, much to the point of deleting the second scene of act 2. Without that scene, as the play stands, Abby may be played as clever and cunning, and the audience decides the depths of her own witchcraft delusions. With the scene in place, she is seen as mad.

Abigail is, however, something more than a romantic adolescent who has been sexually awakened by a mature man. A profitable way to look at Abby is to note that she sees it all as sham, as a "pretense." The critical passage, more significant than heretofore noted, occurs early in the play when, in tears, she says to Proctor, "I never knew what pretense Salem was, I never knew the lying lessons I was taught by all these Christian women and their covenanted men" (24). This revelation to Abby of man's natural depravity and the breadth and depths of secret corruption is an essential ingredient in Puritan thought and is the same discovery that Nathaniel Hawthorne's Young Goodman Brown makes of Salem Village in the story that bears his name. Abigail's response to the discovery is unique to her. She is a moral will-o'-the-wisp, and as such she is deceptive, elusive, and misleading. Each of the other characters in this play believes in something—from Proctor to Danforth, but she believes in nothing. Her life view allows for the manipulation of others. She is a cynic.

Abigail's cynical view of the inhabitants of Salem and of life in general enables her to dance, to perform before them, and then escape. Because they believe, they tend to be serious. Because she sees all people as not only sexual, but evil, she sees goodness and any attempt at goodness as pretense, sham, "lying lessons." She holds the view that all people are corrupt and sinful yet pretend otherwise. Her cynicism allows for no sense of honor; there are no rules to her games, no boundaries she will not cross. In that sense, all of Salem is no match for her. She scorns the rest of society, its interests, and its values. She believes that people are motivated in all their actions entirely by selfishness. "It were sport" (11) is thus her explanation and her justification. In her mind, the word is doubly significant: the dancing in the woods was just a game, but she also believes that life is "sport," that there are no values or goodness, only hypocrisy, nothing that is *normal*. *Sport* is used here not in the sense of recreation, pastime, diversion, or game, but as in biology, denoting a plant or animal showing marked variation from the norm. If life has no norms or mores, anything is possible. Everybody else in this very structured society has a set of rules, but Abigail will observe none.

A "strikingly beautiful girl, an orphan" (8), Abigail lives with Parris, a repressing uncle, who has "no interest in children, or talent with them" (3). While she has little or no sense of honor or community (she has from the first been an outcast and feels herself to be one), Proctor has a heightened sense of honor and an overdeveloped sense of his place in the community. Even if he cannot say all his commandments, he is an intelligent man who is aware of social norms but is impatient with those that seem to him to be sham or counterfeit. Proctor is not one to suffer fools or foolishness gladly. Like Eddie Carbone in *A View from the Bridge,* who knows and respects the codes of conduct of the community and is driven to violate them, Proctor has no time for formulas or pretension. He does not attend church because he will not pretend to ignore what seems to him to be Parris's excesses, rhetorical and financial. His youngest son is not baptized because Proctor sees "no light of God" (65) in Parris. Yet Proctor "is a sinner, a sinner not only against the moral fashion of the time, but against his own vision of decent conduct" (20). Carbone does not, or cannot, accept or acknowledge the nature of the beast within. John Proctor knows perfectly well what he has done.

Proctor is a confident and capable man; he will dispute with Putnam (27–28), is a match for Danforth, and stands up to "the smell" of this authority (31). He is, however, a very human protagonist, hardly too evil or too good, as Bentley would have it. He has a violent temper, which is made manifest in his treatment of Mary Warren (59) and his grabbing Abigail by the hair and pulling her to her feet (109). He can go from a solicitous husband in fairly tender moments with Elizabeth to a man furious with anger. Perhaps his strongest feeling, however, is guilt. He has committed adultery. He does, indeed, still feel attracted to Abby, as Elizabeth observes and he concedes in his confession of lechery to the court.

Several times, Proctor rebuffs the advances of Abigail, but other evidence casts suspicion on how firm his resolve of amendment is. It is the burgeoning and thwarted sexuality of Abby that begins the witch-hunt; it is her cunning and ready wit to defend herself that exacerbates it; but as Proctor begins to perceive her cunning, he feels that he, the denier of witches and witchcraft, the reasonable man, the man of common sense, is guilty not just of adultery but of precipitating the events that decimate Salem. It may occur to Proctor that by that one act in his barn he has set into motion a chain of events he is powerless to restrain or stop. This is the source of his rage, his fury.

9

Arthur Miller and History: The Guilted Ages

I have a sense for heat, John, and yours has drawn me to my window, and I have seen you looking up, burning in your loneliness
—Abigail

Hark ye yet again—the little lower layer.
—Melville, *Moby-Dick*

Arthur Miller has no responsibility to be a historian, of course, but when he makes a point to inform his audience of what he has changed, it seems fair to ask about what he has changed and not told us. His "A Note on the Historical Accuracy of This Play," which serves as a preface to the various editions of *The Crucible,* indicates that the number of individuals in the klatch of pubescent girls has been reduced while Abigail's age has been advanced, and a number of different judges are represented by Hathorne and Danforth. There is no comment about a change in the sequence of events to suit Miller's dramatic purpose. The events in question are the deaths of Proctor and Giles Corey, concerning which an interesting, and significant, change seems to have been made as will be seen in the next chapter.

Miller tells his readers that Abigail's age has been raised but does not elaborate or mention any adjustment in the age of the historical model for John Proctor. Miller's Abigail Williams is 17; most historians place the age of Abigail at 11.[1] Historians are more certain of Procter's age than of Abigail's. In 1692, the historical Procter was 60 years old.[2] Miller's Proctor, however, is "in his middle thirties" (20). In 1953, Arthur Miller was thirty-eight. Some historians say that Miller's Proctor is more fiction than fact; a closer look seems in order.

No one would argue with Miller, who says that the characters in this play "may therefore be taken as creations of my own" (2). As we agree with that, however, we may also agree that "every art work bears to some extent the imprint of the artist's personality, his education, and his experiences."[3]

What does Miller tell us, then, of that period of his life when *The Crucible* was composed? The best source is also the most readily available; his autobiography, *Timebends,* in which he describes his own connections to the play. At one level his remarks are quite enlightening:

> I was researching *The Crucible* . . . I suddenly felt a familiar inner connection with witchcraft and the Puritan cult, its illusions, its stupidities, and its sublimity. . . . I felt strangely at home with these New Englanders, moved in the darkest part of my mind by some instinct that they were putative ur-Hebrews, with the same fierce idealism, devotion to God, tendency to legalistic reductiveness, the same longings for the pure and intellectually elegant argument.
>
> (*Timebends,* 42)

Miller reinforces this cultural association when he writes, "I knew instantly what the connection was: the moral intensity of the Jews and the clan's defensiveness against pollution from outside the ranks. Yes, I understood in that flash, it was suddenly my own inheritance" (*Timebends,* 338).

Yet there may be a more recondite connection at another level for Miller and his play. He remembers that "the theme of the play . . . kept its distance as I groped toward a visceral connection with all this. . . . I knew that my own life was speaking here in many disguises" (*Timebends*, 338). At this time, "in order to save a marriage,"—his own—the dramatist had begun analysis with Rudolph Loewenstein, a Freudian therapist of great skill. Also by this time, Miller had met Marilyn Monroe, and he recalls that his life was havoc. Even after only a few hours, Monroe had taken on an immanence in his imagination. He was struggling to keep his marriage and family together. Miller attempted to maintain the appearances of a confident marriage, but the mutual trust had gone from his relationship with his wife. He continued a warm if sporadic correspondence with the actress. This was the condition of the playwright in the first weeks of thinking about the Salem story when it occurred to him that

> the central image . . . was that of a guilt-ridden man, John Proctor, who, having slept with his teenage servant girl, watches with horror as she becomes the leader of a witch-hunting pack and points her accusing finger at the wife he himself betrayed. . . . And so, in deciding to make an exploratory trip up to Salem, Massachusetts . . . I was moving inward as well as north.
> (*Timebends*, 332)

In the Salem Historical Society building, Miller found "the hard evidence of what had become my play's center: the breakdown of the Proctor marriage and Abigail Williams's determination to get Elizabeth murdered so that she could have John, whom I deduced she had slept with while she was their house servant, before Elizabeth fired her" (*Timebends*, 337). The playwright says he found this in Charles W. Upham's standard history, *Salem Witchcraft* (Boston, 1867). But the Procter Miller discovered in the historical records was sixty years old and Abby was eleven or twelve. May-December romances are possible, but that hardly seems probable between the historical John and Abby.

It was at this point that Miller made the connection between Salem and the political occurrences in Washington, in the fact that both evidenced a "projection of one's own vileness onto others in order to wipe it out with their blood" (*Timebends,* 337). The dramatist may have been projecting a sense of "one's own vileness," however, from a deeper source than the McCarthy hearings. Perhaps Miller's own life was indeed "speaking in many disguises." Of his research at Salem, he concluded that "almost every testimony . . . revealed the sexual theme" (*Timebends,* 340). The guilt of illicit sexuality became a synecdoche for the guilt and shame associated with the House Un-American Activities Committee. Miller knew that guilt and shame were crucial to the workings of the 1950s Red-hunt.[4] Yet Miller says of his own life a short time later: "my soul only half there, but still exhilarated with life and at the same time ridden by guilt" (*Timebends,* 360). Such remarks, taken together, suggest that he was drawing upon his own,—not Procter's—failing marriage and his then still developing relationship with Marilyn Monroe.

There is no denying that the Salem witchcraft trials and the McCarthy witch-hunts were very much on Miller's mind, and in his intentions, during the composition of *The Crucible.* It is not too far-fetched, however, to propose that a third element in the alembic of the composition of the play was the playwright's own life at that time. An author's own psychology is sometimes boggy ground on which to build an analysis or explication of a work of literature. This chapter is *not* meant to explore any Freudian subconscious—where even knowledgeable amateurs ought not venture. Quite to the contrary, this reading does mean to suggest that Miller *consciously* made use of these additional elements. Like many other writers, from Ernest Hemingway to Woody Allen, he may have used the creative process to siphon off the sorrow, energy, elation, and even guilt of a richly creative moment of his life. That he did so is apparent in a careful reading of his autobiography. He knew that his "own life was speaking here."

10

Name

Because it is my name! Because I cannot have another in my life!
—John Proctor

As we have seen, a central leitmotiv of *The Crucible* is John Proctor's concern for his "name." This concern with a name is clarified when placed in the context of Miller's other plays. Joe Keller of *All My Sons,* Willy Loman of *Death of a Salesman,* even Dr. Thomas Stockman in Miller's adaptation of Ibsen's *An Enemy of the People,* are all men concerned, in one way or another, with their reputation or their integrity—the meaning and currency of their name in the society in which they live. An added resonance can be heard in the names of the two best illustrations, which, significantly, come from Miller's plays during the period 1953–55, Eddie Carbone and John Proctor.

His name is so important to him before the neighborhood that Carbone will go fighting like an animal to his death rather than surrender it. As he goes out into the street before the entire assembled neighborhood to meet his death, Eddie cries out directly to his enemy, "Wipin' the neighborhood with my name like a dirty rag! I want my name. . . . Now gimme my name . . ." (*View*, 84). It is not coincidence that Carbone and Proctor are concerned with their name before their neighborhood or their village—in primal terms, their tribe. It is a theme Miller has been articulating since 1941. In a radio fantasy he wrote about a talking cat, Tom, the cat, says, "The one thing a man fears most next to death is the loss of his good name. Man is evil in his own eyes, my friends, worthless."[1]

This "evil in his own eyes" is what resounds in Proctor's being a dozen years later, but by 1953 Miller's protagonists will fear the loss of their good name *more* than death. For the seventeenth-century Puritans, the worst of sins was to lie, which represented a breaking of one's faith, one's reputation, one's "name." But *name* for Miller's characters means not only one's reputation but being true to oneself. Miller feels so strongly about this that at the court acquittal in 1958 of his contempt of Congress charges, he said, "Nobody wants to be a hero . . . but in every man there is something he cannot give up and still remain himself—a core, an identity, a thing that is summed up for him by the sound of his own name on his own ears. If he gives that up, he becomes a different man, not himself" (Nelson, 198). Miller speaks of himself and generalizes to include "every man," but this statement describes John Proctor to a tee.

In point of fact, Proctor's dilemma is a case of art preceding life. Proctor will sign the confession but will not allow it to be made public or used to implicate others. Proctor says, "I speak my own sins; I cannot judge another. . . . I have no tongue for it" (141). The scene (139–42) in which he accepts responsibility for himself but will not name others almost exactly foreshadows what Miller would later do at the House Un-American Activities Committee hearings. The concept of "my name" is intrinsic for Miller as well as his heroes. As a result, Proctor's final temptation, a far greater one than Abigail's lust, is the purchase of his life with the coin of his name.

Why is Proctor, who loves life, willing to die at the end? He has signed the confession but suddenly tears it up. John Proctor is a very human being, a "lecher," who does not want to die. He is not "a little in love with death" like Edmund Tyrone in O'Neill's *Long Day's Journey into Night*. Proctor wants to live. This is why he signs the confession. Why then does he tear it up? Looming large before him are the examples of Rebecca Nurse and Giles Corey. Rebecca, who is brought in at the penultimate moment, is an exemplum of courage and unwavering integrity. She will not lie—that is, compromise her name—and damn herself. Ashamed of what he is doing by signing the confession to save his life, Proctor turns his face to the wall in her presence.

More incisively, Elizabeth innocently tells her husband of Corey's fate (135). Here Miller exercises the greatest dramatic license of the play, and he does so apparently with an eye on his purpose. Historically, John Procter was hanged 19 August 1692; Giles Corey was pressed to death a month later, on 19 September. Miller did not reverse the deaths just so he could include the memorable line "More weight" (135). Whatever Corey's motivation, he would not "give up" or implicate family, friends, and neighbors as Proctor has been asked, but now declines, to do. It is in declining to take the names from his friends that Proctor realizes the importance of his own name, his essential truth, his "honor" (144).

Proctor is reminded by the presence of Rebecca Nurse, who stands ready to die, and by the tale of Giles Corey's death that there are things more important than life, things worth dying for. Reverend Hale, who has gone through his own catharsis, now presents the view that "life is God's most precious gift; no principle, however glorious, may justify the taking of it" (132). Proctor knows better. Hale insists that Elizabeth plead with him, seeing Proctor's act as "pride . . . vanity" (145). Proctor passes from the crucible of his test, but the temptation for the audience might be to see in Proctor a tragic flaw, to suspect that like the heroes of old, he suffers from hubris. In the final analysis, however, his name is more important than his pride. Proctor is willing to die because he has been reminded that there are values greater than life. Here the play, specifically about both Salem and the 1950s, broaches its most universal and human, matter, and the drama opens up to involve the audience and the readers themselves.

Rather than fade into a historical piece, the play is produced more and more and is read by a larger and larger audience. Why? As values, other than those placed on material things, decline, young audiences seem to embrace John Proctor and endorse his actions. He has value because he has values—beyond material things and his own selfishness. He is no aesthete or ethereal philosopher. He is a man of his time who transcends time and seems, in some ways, a curiously contemporary man. Proctor wants a god, not a church of gold candlesticks; he enjoys hard work and his property; he is a full-blooded sexual being who loves flesh and the things of this world, from a good stew to the flowers in his fields. Yet he will give all of these things up— and his own life—because he has a sense of honor, integrity, and justice. Proctor says that he is "no saint" (138), yet perhaps he haunts the American imagination because he is as close as this nation comes to providing a model for sainthood—one who places values above his own well-being and is willing to suffer martyrdom in the interest of his fellow man. Arthur Miller has said as recently as 1989 that what he hoped *The Crucible* would demonstrate to the country and to the world "was the continuity through time of human delusion, and the only safeguard, fragile though it may be, against it—namely, the law and the courageous few whose sacrifice illuminates delusion" ("Again They Drink," 36).

John Proctor, the play in which he is the protagonist, and its author are among those courageous few who do illuminate our delusions.

11

Triangles

triangle (trī´aŋ g'l), *n.* [ME.; OFr.; L. *triangulum;* see tri- & angle],
1. a geometrical figure having three angles and three sides. 2. a group
of three involved in some situation, as one in which two men are in
love with the same woman.

It is interesting to reexamine *The Crucible* in the context of the two
adjacent major plays in the Miller canon, *Death of a Salesman* (1949)
and *A View from the Bridge* (1956). In this seven-year span, the playwright, at the peak of his powers, wrote three plays that are quite dis-
similar in content and theme, yet each play contains a marital and
sexual triangle.

A brief recollection of Miller's own biography is germane and
suggestive here. In 1940, Miller married his college sweetheart, Mary
Grace Slattery. His first real celebrity came to him in 1947 with *All My
Sons,* and on a trip to California in 1950 the dramatist met Marilyn
Monroe, not a year after the premiere of *Death of a Salesman.*
Although he remained married, a warm relationship developed
between the playwright and the motion-picture star. As has already
been seen, Miller's personal relationships became increasingly difficult

and uncomfortable. In 1953 *The Crucible* premiered, and shortly thereafter, in 1955, Monroe moved to New York City. What followed in short order was Miller's Reno divorce and his marriage to Monroe. Miller accompanied her to England for the filming of Terence Rattigan's *The Prince and The Showgirl* and the debut of the two-act version of *A View from the Bridge* directed by Peter Brook. The Miller-Monroe marriage would last until a 1961 divorce; Miller would then marry for a third time, this time to Inge Morath. Miller's next major work, the screenplay for *The Misfits,* would not come until 1961, during the dissolution of his relationship with Monroe. His next play, *After the Fall,* according to some critics, celebrates that dissolution. The two subsequent plays, *Incident at Vichy* and *The Price,* do not contain love triangles.

In examining Miller's personal and professional experiences from 1949 to 1956, it becomes clear that this was the most turbulent and tumultuous time of his life. Yet, despite all the political furor and personal angst, indeed perhaps *because* of them, it is even clearer that Miller was at what may be seen now as the peak of his power as a playwright. In this time, he wrote his best three plays, all of which include triangles of "other" women coming between long-suffering wives and their philandering, wayward, or lost husbands. The triangles in Miller's best plays always consist of one man and two women, never one woman and two men. In *Death of a Salesman,* produced before Miller's first divorce, the triangle is not serious as it applies to Linda or Willy and "The Woman" directly but as it affects Biff and his relationship with his father, and most especially, as it haunts Willy's reverie. As Miller's personal life grew more complicated, the triangle of John Proctor, Elizabeth, and Abigail in *The Crucible* grows more serious. It is the triangle of Eddie Carbone, his wife Beatrice, and their niece Catherine that may appear the most verboten and devastating, even if it is an unrealized or incomplete sexual triangle.

The primary matter to be considered here, however, is how one's perspective on the triangle in *The Crucible* changes in the light of the major play preceding it and the major play following it. As we have seen, Miller himself felt that the commercial failure of the first production of *The Crucible* was due to the fact that the play's original director, Jed Harris, had neglected the prime importance of the theme of illicit sexuality and its residual guilt. Stated most simply, Harris underestimated the importance of the romantic and sexual triangle represented by Proctor, Elizabeth, and Abigail. Because of Miller's sensitive depiction of human motivation and his understanding and sympathy for those caught within the bounds of the triangle, it would seem, at first glance, that there is no "right" angle to this triangle. To fully understand the triangle portrayed in *The Crucible,* perhaps one must reflect back on an almost invisible triangle, that in *Death of a Salesman.*

The woman with whom Willy Loman has allowed a playful flirtation to develop into a recurrent rendezvous never appears in the present of the play and exists only in Willy's memory. If she is part of Willy's sense of guilt, it is not for his adultery: on the contrary, her significance is primarily as a reminder of Willy's larger sense of failure. The woman's laughter is first heard, and then she is dimly seen, in the play's first act in a scene in which Linda, Willy's wife, is darning stockings.[1] It is not explicitly sexual guilt that sets off Willy's recollection but the fact that he remembers having given the woman gifts of stockings because Linda sits before him "mending a pair of her silk stockings" (39). It is his guilt, not as an adulterer but as a failed provider that causes him to say, "I'll make it all up to you, Linda" (39) and then angrily explode: "I won't have you mending stockings in this house! Now throw them out!" (39). If Loman is not constant, he is consistent. If he has been unfaithful to his wife, he is faithful to his dream.

Linda, far from throwing them out, ignores his demand and puts the stockings into her pocket. The stockings are an obvious, perhaps too obvious, signature and symbol. As Linda removes them from sight, the woman's laugh fades away and the play returns to its present. The woman will not return to the play until the climactic scene in act 2 when Biff's failure to meet with Bill Oliver and his subsequent theft of Oliver's fountain pen stir Willy to recall Biff's high school failure in mathematics and Biff's pursuit of Willy to Boston, where Willy's relationship with the woman is revealed to the audience. This scene

(111–21) is a major revelation in the play, but not as an indication of a single source of the separation of Biff and Willy or of a son's disillusionment with his father, but as an exposition of what troubles Willy. It is, after all, completely in the past, and appears in Willy's recollection. Members of the audience must continually remind themselves that the scenes of the past all occur in Willy's imaginings. In Miller's opinion and in his intention, these scenes—with the exception of the "Requiem" (which explains why it must be a separate coda)—are not flashbacks but occur for Loman in "the inside of his head" (which was Miller's title for the working draft of the play). There is no clear-cut sense of sexual guilt inside Willy's head—the philandering father caught in a hotel room with a partially clad woman by a distraught son seeking a palliative for his own failure. What troubles Willy as he moves toward the play's conclusion really is not that he has done it, but that it reminds him of that which he has deprived Linda. The woman does not appear again, nor is her laughter heard in the play's last 15 pages—nor is there so much as a hint of her in the play's final "Requiem" (137–39).

Loman's rationale and explanation to Biff of his illicit relationship with the woman he calls Miss Francis is that he is lonely: "She's nothing to me, Biff. I was lonely, I was terribly lonely" (120). This is not a stereotypical traveling salesman joke; Willy Loman certainly loves his wife, and it is not a case of his loving the girl he is with when he is not with the girl he loves. Indeed, his own values, his own distorted ambitions, contribute to his existential loneliness. Yet Linda shares those values.

Linda Loman is Willy's defender and apologist and remains so until the end; there is no solid evidence that she ever knows of Willy's road-show romances. When the reader first meets Linda, she is described as having "developed an iron repression of her expectations to Willy's behavior—she more than loves him, she admires him, as though his mercurial nature, his temper, his massive dreams and little cruelties, served her only as sharp reminders of the turbulent longings within him, longings which she shares" (12). Traces in Linda of intense materialism have inspired inventive critics and scholars to see Linda *as*

"The Woman," or at least behaving in league with her and helping to drive Willy toward suicide.[2] Yet it would be misleading to identify Linda too closely with "The Woman." Linda "more than loves" her Willy. She has no idea of Willy's assignations, and she is caught up in the same "massive dreams." This last point is made evident in the play's final words—spoken by Linda: "I can't understand it, Willy. I made the last payment on the house today. Today, dear. . . . We're free and clear. . . . We're free . . ." (139).

What *is* clear is that Linda is better seen when she is identified with Willy, not the woman, and that the sexual triangle is *not* crucial to the major dynamics of this play or to the story of Willy Loman. This triangle is really unessential; yes, it must be conceded that it changes things for the adolescent Biff—or, properly, Willy's projected imaginings in retrospect, which is all the audience has access to—to find his father in the Standish Arms with the woman, but if it had not been that it could have or would have been something else. The audience has no direct access in those scenes set in the past to what Biff is thinking, only to what Willy thinks Biff thought or must have thought. For if this is only about a young man's grievance on finding that his father indulged in sexual escapades, then *Death of a Salesman* is less, much less, of a play. Willy's grief and what bothers Biff run much deeper. Unlike his brother Happy, Biff does not have his father's vision and does not want to be like his father. He loves his father and always has, but he does not believe in his broader "massive" dreams. Thus he concludes of his father: "He had the wrong dreams. All, all, wrong" (138). Biff has learned from his father's experience what and who he, Biff, is not, but his father cannot learn from his son to "take that phony dream and burn it" (133). It is a dream as broad and enduring as the American continent. Therefore, the triangle, while dramatically valid, is not essential to Miller's principal concern here. The play is not satisfying if it is about a son's discovery of a father's failings—that play Miller had already written in *All My Sons*. *Death of a Salesman* deals with far more than that, perhaps best characterized in Willy's final misled encomium; as he attempts to plant seed by the light of a flashlight, he says, "A man can't go out the way he came in . . . a man has got to add up to something" (125). What Willy doesn't know (which John Proctor will) is precisely that a man *does* "go out" as he came in—and what he adds up to in his lifetime is not an accumulation of *things*. All refrigerators break down. So do cars—even better cars than a Studebaker.

If Linda Loman is a wife who does not know about the triangle of which she has been a part, Beatrice Carbone in *A View from the Bridge* recognizes a triangle of which her husband seems consciously unaware and in which he is trapped. Like *The Crucible* and *Death of a Salesman, A View from the Bridge*, while it contains a three-sided marital complication, is not a play "about" a triangle. It is Miller's most underestimated play; if there is one play that seems destined to grow in coming years in popular response and academic appreciation, it is *A View from the Bridge*. Far from merely examining a narrow relationship of three people, it is a play of fierce power and extraordinary theatricality, a serious and mature play about the differences between the law and justice, dramatized through a conflict between two physically superior men, and providing remarkable insights into the complex, often unrecognized, motives that move the human animal. Moreover, it is both an insightful treatment of loyalty, familial relationships, and class values and a near-perfect case study of an individual and his ethnic and socioeconomic class. For all of this, it is still the triangle that best provides the contrasting substance and allows another way to study and diagnose the relationships within *The Crucible*. The triangle in *A View from the Bridge* is formed by Eddie Carbone, his wife, Beatrice, and Beatrice's niece Catherine, who has been raised by the Carbones.

At first blush, the sexual aberration in *A View from the Bridge* seems the most significant and troubling in the entire Miller canon because it leads most directly to the death of the play's central protagonist. Even worse, it deals with something far more profound than a man's infidelity. If adultery will be seen by some viewers as falling in the shadowy outskirts of acceptable social behavior, incest—real or potential—sits in the dark middle of an anthropological cave of forbidden activity. This is not merely legal transgression or moral violation, but, in most modern societies, an essential tribal taboo, older than the human development of laws or ethics. Thus, while Eddie may be consciously unaware of it, the implications of his potential for incest are profound. Miller works this play in the most basic colors of the human emotions, and his principal players move with savage and primitive intensity.

In broader terms, consider the reactions of each of the nine characters in the plays under consideration to the web of intrigue in which they have become entangled. To begin, consider the responses of the three wives in the plays. Linda Loman is overtly unaware of the existence of the other woman and oblivious to the implications the memories have for Willy. Elizabeth Proctor's role is far more difficult. She not only is keenly aware of the existence of the triangle and its residual effects, recognizing the serious implications that Abigail's relationship with John has for him in his own development, but also must grow to accept, and articulate to her husband, her own sense of culpability in the matter.

Beatrice Carbone, on the other hand, is aware of the potential danger in Eddie's relationship with Catherine. Miller's revision of *A View from the Bridge,* which made it a full-length play, was achieved principally by expanding the character and viewpoint of Beatrice. In her complex emotions, the audience sees her as both a properly concerned aunt and, as she admits, a woman "jealous" of Eddie's attention to Catherine. In a sharply focused scene in act 1 between Catherine and Beatrice, she warns her niece that she cannot continue to act as she has in the past: "You still walk around in front of him in your slip—. . . Or like you sit on the edge of the bathtub talkin' to him when he's shavin' in his underwear. . . . you're a grown woman and you're in the same house with a grown man. So you'll act different now, heh?" (*View,* 40–41). Shortly thereafter, the richly complex, very human Beatrice, both relative and rival, warns her niece that she should have thought of her jealousy before:

> BEATRICE:. . . he should let you go. But, you see, if only I tell
> him, he thinks I'm just bawlin' him out, or maybe I'm jealous
> or somethin', you know?
> CATHERINE, *astonished:* He said you was jealous?

> BEATRICE: No, I'm just sayin' maybe that's what he thinks. *She reaches over to Catherine's hand; with a strained smile:* You think I'm jealous of you, honey?
> CATHERINE: No! It's the first I thought of it.
> BEATRICE, *with a quiet sad laugh:* Well you should have thought of it before . . . (*View,* 41)

Seen against Beatrice, this later creation of Miller, Elizabeth Proctor stands out more clearly in both her strengths and her shortcomings.

Quite as informative is a comparison of the third persons in the triangles. The involvement of the other woman in the earlier *Death of a Salesman* is desultory, unlike Catherine's, which is more serious, and Abby's, which is deadly. The woman in *Death of a Salesman* sees the affair with Willy pretty much as Willy sees it. Willy didn't "make" her (her word); she picked him, and she did so because he had a sense of humor and they had such a good time together (*Salesman,* 38). She expects nothing more than that—that, and "a lot of stockings" (*Salesman,* 39). For his part, she can put him "right through to the buyers" (*Salesman,* 116). Willy Loman is self-centered, "the saddest, self-centeredest soul I ever did see-saw" (*Salesman,* 116), as the woman titillatingly chides him. Willy playfully slaps her bottom, and he may grab her and kiss her roughly (*Salesman,* 39), but neither one expects anything beyond "the middle of the night" (*Salesman,* 116) in the form of an enduring or protracted personal relationship. The next day, it will be the professional, practical, and material advantages of the silk stockings for her and the *open sesame* to the buyers for him. The relationship is consistent with Willy's character throughout the play, and it is part of how his persona is revealed to the audience. This triangle has three sides but no depth.

Catherine in *A View from the Bridge* is as innocent as a 17-year-old girl raised by an overly protective Italian-American uncle at that time and in that neighborhood of Red Hook should be. To Miller's understanding, she would be as incapable of an actual incestuous act as her troubled uncle. Yet she is neither stupid nor unaware. Beatrice has warned her, but if Beatrice's complexity of character allows her to be both aunt and rival—and it does—Catherine is as complex. In her conversation about Beatrice with Rodolpho (her young immigrant sweetheart, to whose courtship Eddie objects so vehemently), Catherine sounds as much wife as niece:

> Beatrice says to be a woman. . . . Then why don't she be a woman? If I was a wife I would make a man happy instead of goin' at him all the time. I can tell a block away when he's blue in his mind and just wants to talk to somebody quiet and nice. . . . I can tell when he's hungry or wants a beer before he even says anything. I know when his feet hurt him, I mean I *know* him and now I'm supposed to turn around and make a stranger out of him?
>
> (*View,* 61)

The audience is moved to sympathy for all three persons locked in the situation unfolded here. That is not the case with *The Crucible,* yet that is not a flaw in the play or an oversight on the part of the dramatist. Abigail Williams is not a sympathetic character, nor can she be. She is a memorable theatrical creation exactly because—her being an orphan notwithstanding—she is the cynic, with no values, no honor.

Elizabeth Proctor and Beatrice Carbone, despite the apparent insularity of their roles as homemakers—an occupation they share with Linda Loman—are both astute judges of human character and relationships. Elizabeth, like Beatrice, knows her husband's desires. Elizabeth is even more clearly seen in contrast to Linda, who also knows her husband's desires but is so concomitantly caught up in them that she appears to lack the dynamic growth of John Proctor's wife, even as Linda remains a sympathetic character. Elizabeth comes to self-realization, but Linda is left to repeat over and over, "I can't understand it" (*Salesman,* 137, 138, 139).

As Willy's involvement in his triangle is apropos to his character and situation, the triangle in *A View from the Bridge* is passionately emotional, quivering at the edge of an underlying physicality apposite for the ethnic and socioeconomic milieu of that play's characters. The same social and historical veritas holds for the triangle in *The Crucible.* Despite the development of the six women in the triangles and the thread of the guilt of illicit sexuality, however, each play focuses not on its women but on its male protagonist.

The men's parts in the triangles serve to reveal qualities essential to an audience's understanding of their characters. Willy is apparently unregenerate because his is a recollection of an affair long in the past, for which he feels little sexual guilt. Eddie Carbone is driven by a monster he can neither recognize nor accept. When he consults Alfieri, the lawyer, he is told to let his niece go, for she can't marry him; Eddie responds furiously, "What're you talkin' about, marry me! I don't know what the hell you're talkin' about!" (*View*, 47). Even when Beatrice, desperate to prevent the bloodshed with which the play ends, openly accuses Eddie of harboring incestuous desires, Eddie's honest response is to clench his fists to "his head as though it will burst," and cry out in agony: "that's what you think of me—that I would have such a thought?" (*View*, 84). That Eddie knows and respects the neighborhood code of the deaf and dumb is made abundantly clear in his reaction to the story told in act 1 about Vinny Bolzano, the neighborhood young man who "snitched" to the Immigration Bureau. Despite this, Eddie is being driven to violate every code he believes in, driven by forces he cannot understand. Thus, his penultimate words as he dies are "Then why—" (*View*, 85). Why? Eddie never understands his own nature. The view is not merely of the slum on the seaward side of the Brooklyn Bridge but from the bridge, ancient as it is, of civilization, and Eddie is that species of throwback who has no means or faculties to understand his own motives and drives. He is, then, what Marco calls him as he turns the blade inward and presses it home into Eddie: "Animal!" (*View*, 85). Unschooled, unlettered, unsophisticated, and essentially uncivilized, Eddie will not compromise, will not settle for half, and is reduced to what is most basic and elemental—an animal. Miller's creation reminds us that if the animal is not the prettiest or most noble part of us, it *is* nevertheless part of us. What moves us as we watch Eddie, and what wins us, like Alfieri, to his side at last is that we recognize in Eddie our own inability, no matter where we are on the bridge of civilization, to know completely who we are or, often, why we do what we do. Of such stuff are ancient tragedies made.

If *A View from the Bridge* and *The Crucible* may be seen as tragedies, a matter to be considered in detail later, it is because Eddie and John Proctor are in some ways like Hamlet, powerless to stop a chain of events that they have set in motion. In his first pass at attempting to kill Claudius, Hamlet inadvertently kills Polonius, the act from which all else will follow. Thus, once Eddie calls the Immigration Bureau, even though he later tries to stop them and to minimize the consequences, the events leading to the catastrophe follow as though preordained. The audiences—like the viewers of the action in *The Crucible* or the chorus in Greek drama, and like Alfieri, a modern Greek chorus—sit "there powerless . . . and watched it run its bloody course" (*View*, 5). Yet Eddie never knows why what has happened did in fact happen. And here, comparisons are not odious, but profitable. Seen against Willy Loman and Eddie Carbone, both great dramatic and literary creations, John Proctor seems to stand even taller.

While society ordinarily does not condone infidelity or countenance adultery, they are not hanging matters. It takes a long time, but eventually Elizabeth Proctor accepts her responsibility in the formation of the triangle, and by the play's conclusion she can accept what has happened as she could not as late as act 2. Moreover, she can forgive her wayward, philandering husband.

But can he forgive himself? Proctor needs more than the forgiveness of Elizabeth. Since his sin is against his own sense of what is right, it is more difficult for him to come to expiation. What was his sin? Examined in the light of the failures of Willy Loman and Eddie Carbone, Proctor is a full-blooded, sexual being whose initial sin is his humanity, a healthy, if forbidden, fall into his own human concupiscence.

The fact is that Proctor's greater guilt is that he allows his sexual guilt to hold him powerless for a time to stem the disaster. Proctor knows that his guilt goes beyond illicit sexuality: that only confirms his humanity. The true sin is his reluctance and tardiness in accepting his communal responsibility, which denigrates that same humanity. The significance of his dilemma, and the faltering initial attempts at a proper course of action? Eddie Carbone does not know; Proctor knows and knows better. His guilt goes beyond the extramarital triangle, and thus he is a greater sinner than Willy or Eddie. The trio of Proctor, Elizabeth, and Abigail is of deeper significance because of its rippling effect on the social fabric of Salem. Willy's flirtations and philandering actions haunt him. Eddie's incestuous desires, unrealized and unrecognized, destroy him. The chain of events set in motion by Proctor's infidelity is far greater and his response to it is heroic.

12

Tragedy

One finds, I suppose, what one seeks.
—Introduction to *Arthur Miller's Collected Plays*

John Proctor is "heroic" not merely because he points the finger at himself, but because his story allows him to point out the evil in his environment, the enemy of man's freedom, here the repressive structures of society that would take a man's name. Yet there is more to it than that. As late as 10 years after the initial performance of *The Crucible,* Miller himself wrote that "the mission of writing is tragedy. . . . I believe at bottom, that the word has not yet entered the blood stream of America because it is a country which as yet has no tragic sense of itself."[1]

The question of whether *The Crucible* is tragedy has been hotly debated.[2] The bulk of criticism on the drama centers upon it as a "social play," but there have been continuing attempts to define and redefine its genre. At its premiere, the reviewer for the *New Leader,* for one, called it a melodrama.[3] One of the best of the Miller scholars, Gerald Weales, however, forces the reader's focus to *The Crucible:* "Is it a tragedy in the traditional sense of the word? . . . Does *The Crucible* meet those conditions laid down by Aristotle? Has John Proctor the stature we demand of a tragic hero?" (Weales, 476). In short, is the play a tragedy? If so, in whose terms—Aristotle's? Miller's?

One of the most obvious difficulties in establishing whether Miller's play is a tragedy is to decide on a satisfactory definition of the term. This is no place to attempt to resolve the question of what defines a tragedy, but we ought briefly to survey the traditional dilemmas in arriving at a viable definition of tragedy; then, if there is no mutually agreed upon consensus as to what defines tragedy in drama, it may be fair to measure *The Crucible* by Miller's own definitions of the genre.

In the eighteenth century, the British writer Horace Walpole (1717–97) craftily observed that "the world is a comedy to those that think, a tragedy to those that feel."[4] Or, in contemporary parlance, comedy is when someone else slips and falls on a banana peel; tragedy is when *you* do. Likewise, to agree that Aristotle declared drama to be separate from other sorts of imaginative literature because the playwright presents his characters living and moving before an audience and that tragedies end unhappily while comedies end happily is too much of an oversimplified distinction to be useful. Perhaps the best balance between sophistication, common sense, and clarity of articulation tells us:

> According to Aristotle, whose definition in the *Poetics* is an inductive description of the Greek tragedies, the purpose of a tragedy is to arouse the emotions of pity and fear and thus to produce in the audience a catharsis of these emotions. . . . The question of the nature of the significance of the tragic hero is answered in each age by the concept of significance that is held by that age. In a period of monarchy, Shakespeare's protagonists were kings and rulers; in other ages they have been and will be other kinds of men. In a democratic nation, founded on an egalitarian concept of man, a tragic hero can be the archetypal common man . . . a New England farmer.[5]

For all of this, it remains more than a simple, or resolved, matter in the minds of many. Critics and scholars disagree not only about how Aristotle's tenets might be applied to Miller's drama, but also about what

Aristotle's *Poetics* says and means. Perhaps the most manageable digest version of Aristotle's requirements for tragedy is supplied by Alan A. Stambusky. The six principal points include that the play's action must apply to the experience of all men and not be restricted to one particular person; the plot must not be narrative but dramatic and of a "magnitude" that is genuinely significant; and to be considered tragic, the hero must be a highly moral individual who has a tragic flaw, a hamartia. This flaw is often hubris—commonly characterized as pride—which is best thought of as a person's disposition to go beyond the limits prescribed by accepted social order. Moreover, Aristotle would expect a complex plot containing a reversal of circumstances, or peripeteia, and a complete recognition of the significance of the hero's action, an *anagnorisis*, by the hero and the audience. The last principles would be that plot be considered more important than character, and the drama's language be pleasurable whether it be prose or poetry.

These are the general characteristics of a Greek tragedy; the best-known intention of the drama, essential to Aristotle, is that the drama succeed in achieving a particular effect, the purgation of the soul by pity and fear. A perfectly good person—take Rebecca Nurse as an example—would be disqualified as a fit tragic hero because suffering that is unjustified arouses repulsion rather than fear and pity. As well, the converse would be true; someone who is morally corrupt cannot be a tragic persona because a reversal of fortune in this case would awaken no pity. Thus, the tragic hero is not a naive or singularly virtuous person, but a good human being whose misfortune is brought on him or her not by vice but by an error in judgment:

> The ideal protagonist of tragedy, then, says Aristotle, must be a man like ourselves, one who does not possess righteousness and virtue *to perfection,* but whose character is held in high esteem by all. In other words, the tragic character will have the same characteristics possessed by all mankind, but these characteristics will be "larger than life," of greater scope than those displayed by ordinary men; he will be more brave, strong-willed, or magnanimous than ordinary persons.
>
> (Stambusky, 92)

As has been suggested above, it is not a requisite of tragedy that the hero be a king or a prince. The oft-noted fall from high to low refers primarily to morality and intellect, not social position or wealth. Perhaps the notion that the fall must be of a person of noble social station, springing from Greek and Renaissance concepts, is further fed by Puritan and indigenous American springs—that, following the Protestant ethic, a person is better than his neighbors or other citizens because of economic and social prosperity or that prestige and material acquisition are indicative of the blessings of God or the favor of the gods. Recall that

> the history of the drama has included three great tragic periods, the England of Shakespeare, the Athens of Sophocles, and the France of Corneille and Racine. . . . Basic to tragedy is an order of values which transcends man and which man should obey. Among the Greeks this order rested on the notion of fate, among the Elizabethans on the notion of a highly structured universe in which the individual's place is determined, and among the French classical writers on the concept of honor and duty.
>
> (Bain, 584)

It remained for Arthur Miller to bring the theory of tragedy into the twentieth century and the United States.

How would John Proctor fare, however, if he were to be appraised by Aristotelian measures? The play's action, first of all, is universal, applying to the lives of the entire community and not necessarily to one particular man. The historic events of 1692 and the 1950s make that fact eminently conspicuous. The plot of *The Crucible* is dramatic, complete, and unified. Its magnitude is grand (indeed, as shall be seen later, it is operatic) and is not only serious but has been faulted for being unrelievedly so. The play's hero is of generally high moral character and his downfall may be placed at the feet of his tragic flaw. Aristotle held that: "This error or frailty which constitutes the hero's tragic flaw consists in some moral defect inherent in the tragic hero's character which leads him, when the chips are down, to consciously and intentionally err in judgment and thereby commit some wrong act" (Stambusky, 93).

This deep-seated disposition or "frailty" is Proctor's own essential humanity and demonstrates him to be "a man like ourselves." And since this is so, the resultant catharsis arouses, and purges, our own pity and fear.

Does the play reveal a peripeteia? Proctor's reversal of circumstances has been too fully documented earlier to need elaboration or further comment here. And Proctor does exceed the limits of the then accepted social order, so much so, that, as has been seen, Parris and Danforth respond as they do, in part, because Proctor's challenge shakes the very social structure supporting the minister's and Deputy Governor's position and power.

As for an *anagnorisis,* that is a matter both simple and complex. John Proctor certainly and clearly achieves his profound recognition. Miller had especially chosen his ambience with this in mind. He has said, "In *The Crucible* I had taken a step, I felt, toward a more self-aware drama. The Puritan not only felt, but constantly referred his feelings to concepts, to codes and ideas of social and ethical importance" (*View,* vi–vii). This tragic self-awareness is the sine qua non to Proctor's situation and character. On the other hand, whether that *anagnorisis* can be said to apply to the unraveling or denouement of the dramatic plot to an audience is a thornier matter. One supposes that, as in all things, it depends upon the individual audience.

One of the principal Aristotelian tenets for tragedy would disqualify *The Crucible:* that character be held secondary to plot. As we have seen, Miller has not built his play in that fashion. Finally, there is the matter of language. Far from being stilted or awkward, as some critics contend, the language of *The Crucible* is elevated and poetic. Miller himself says, "I often write speeches in verse, and then break them down. . . . *The Crucible* was all written in verse, but I broke it up" (*Essays,* 277–78). In point of fact, one of the dangers in reading Miller's plays—as opposed to seeing them in production—is to find the dialogue and patois rudimentary or commonplace. Quite the contrary, the argot of Joe Keller or Willy Loman and the street-wise level of diction of Eddie Carbone, but especially the language of John Proctor, can at the same time be true to the demands of verisimilitude and qualify as poetic language.

On the other hand, to limit an appreciation of Miller's contemporary tragedy because it does not align with each of the Renaissance conceptions of tragedy or with all the dicta of Aristotle's *Poetics* is to ignore the uniqueness of historical period. Each age must, as Emerson says, write its own books: the rubrics of one age do not fit another. In its broadest definition, a tragedy depicts a series of important events in the life of a person; the diction is elevated, the play's progression is serious or dignified, and its resolution is catastrophic. It is a drama of lofty intent and deals, most often, with the darker side of life and human nature. All of this may be said to apply to *The Crucible*.

There is, however, still another area to be explored. Arthur Miller has written more about his own plays than other American writers have written about theirs. He is, as has already been suggested, a skilled essayist and an astute and perceptive theater critic.

> What makes Miller such an excellent essayist is not merely that he is so sound and perceptive . . . but [that his] thoughts are . . . accessible. His prose is clear and direct; he says what he thinks and though his prose is graceful, often poetic, it is never obscure, obstruent, or abstruse. Miller's essays are valuable because they reveal him to be a humanistic and humane human being concerned with the "community" of the theater and the world, and they express his vision clearly. . . . The reader does not have to search through rhetorical evasiveness and excesses or ponderous prose that might hide an indecision or indecisiveness. Miller is . . . clear, intelligent, intelligible and . . . accessible to the reader.
>
> (Martine, xi)

What does Miller expect of tragedy? Without question, he insists that the common man is as qualified a subject for tragedy in its highest sense as kings and princes. In his first and most famous essay on the topic, "Tragedy and the Common Man," he posits that "the tragic feeling is evoked in us when we are in the presence of a character who is ready to lay down his life, if need be, to secure one thing—his sense of personal dignity" (*Essays,* 4). Written 48 months before *The Crucible,* these lines apply to John Proctor as much as they might to

Orestes, Hamlet, Medea, or Macbeth. Moreover, Miller explains that "tragedy, then, is the consequence of a man's total compulsion to evaluate himself justly. . . . The flaw, or crack in the character, is really nothing—and need be nothing—but his inherent unwillingness to remain passive in the face of what he conceives to be a challenge to his dignity, his image of his rightful status" (*Essays*, 4). John Proctor, who could not have been in Miller's mind as he wrote these lines in 1949, spends one act and part of another almost passive, but once he perceives the nature of the challenge to his dignity and the damage to his own image of his rightful status—summed up for him in his name—he comes to a decision and acts decisively. Moreover, the playwright is almost prescient in his anticipation of his witchcraft play, which will come four years later, when he concludes that "tragedy enlightens . . . in that it points the heroic finger at the enemy of man's freedom. The thrust for freedom is the quality in tragedy which exalts" (*Essays*, 5). What this means eventually, of course, is that Miller's drama holds up well when scrutinized in the looking-glass of his personal theory of what constitutes tragedy. But when he concludes "it is time . . . that we who are without kings, took up this bright thread of our history and followed it to the only place it can possibly lead in our time—the heart and spirit of the average man" (*Essays*, 7), it is a call that is as much national as personal.

Exactly one month later, the dramatist would return to his subject with "The Nature of Tragedy," which acknowledges that there are entire libraries dealing with the subject, and he concedes that the idea of tragedy is constantly changing. Yet he finds a residual core of permanence:

> When I show you why a man does what he does, I may do so melodramatically; but when I show why he almost did not do it, I am making drama. . . . as soon as one investigates not only why a man is acting, but what is trying to prevent him from acting . . . it becomes extremely difficult to contain the action in the forced and arbitrary form of melodrama.
>
> (*Essays*, 8–9)

Indeed, some of the most intense drama in *The Crucible* is devoted exactly to why John Proctor "almost did not do" what he did. Miller explains that for him "the essential difference, and the precise difference between tragedy and pathos is that tragedy brings . . . us knowledge or enlightenment" (*Essays*, 9). The milieu of *The Crucible* is not just the dawning of the new sun "pouring in" at the play's conclusion (145), but the dawn of a new age of enlightenment. Yet what sort of knowledge does the play bring us? Miller contends that "there is some good in the worst of us" (*Essays*, 10), and John Proctor is not among the worst of us but among the best of us. Miller believes that "tragedy arises when we are in the presence of a man who has missed accomplishing his joy. But the joy must be there, the promise of the right way of life must be there. . . . In a word, tragedy is the most accurately balanced portrayal of the human being in his struggle for happiness." (*Essays*, 11). John Proctor indeed misses accomplishing his joy, and the final act certainly suggests that the right way of life was there. A careful reader and attentive audience of *The Crucible* understands fully that for Miller, "tragedy . . . is the most perfect means we have of showing us who and what we are, and what we must be—or strive to become" (*Essays*, 11).

In his introduction to the *Collected Plays,* Miller has his most lengthy say on *The Crucible,* and he reiterates, "it is necessary, if one is to reflect reality, not only to depict why a man does what he does, or why he nearly didn't do it, but why he cannot simply walk away and say to hell with it" (*Essays*, 117). This describes John Proctor and why he did not take his family and just escape Salem, as historically some others had done. Miller knows "there is an extraordinarily small number of conflicts which we must, at any cost, live out to their conclusions" (*Essays*, 117). Proctor is a man who lives out a conflict to its conclusion. He is a person like us in that he has "some value, some challenge, however minor or major, which he cannot find it in himself to walk away from or turn his back on" (*Essays*, 118). It has been said that every man has his price, something he will not do or allow to happen under any circumstances. In John Proctor, Miller captures

> that moment of commitment . . . that moment when, in my
> eyes, a man differentiates himself from every other man, that

moment when out of a sky full of stars he fixes on one star. . . .
the less capable a man is of walking away from the central conflict of the play, the closer he approaches a tragic existence. In
turn, this implies that the closer a man approaches tragedy the
more intense is his concentration upon the fixed point of his
commitment.

(*Essays,* 118)

Arthur Miller argues that the assumption behind all his plays,
including *The Crucible,* "is that life has meaning" (*Essays,* 119). It is
the nonnegotiable element in each of his plays and in his essays. For
this reason alone, one would be disposed to agree with Stambusky,
who concludes that "in this one respect, that he believes in the essential worth and dignity of man, Arthur Miller now is closer to the
ancient tragic concept than any of his leading American contempo-
raries" (117).

In a 1966 interview, Miller was asked if he considered his
plays modern tragedies. He responded that he had changed his mind
about it several times, and felt that any direct or arithmetical comparison to the classic tragedies was impossible (*Essays,* 266). On the
other hand, Miller insists that "*The Crucible* is, internally,
Salesman's blood brother" (*Essays,* 172–73), but that the big difference is that *The Crucible* includes a higher degree of consciousness
than the earlier plays. No matter which theory of what constitutes a
tragedy a reader eventually develops—and readers must, it seems,
develop their own tenets, suitable to them and their age—it would
appear that one of the essential components must be this self-awareness on the part of the hero. That Oedipus kills Laius and marries
Jocasta can be pathetic. That he discovers and knows what he has
done is tragic. Thus, John Proctor is heroic because he accepts his
guilt and indicts the society that would force him to give over his
conscience. To do both, he must be self-discovered, self-recognized,
and finally self-accepting.

Ultimately, however, it might be said that an excessive concern
for and abstract arguments about genre obscure the more important
elements in the play and lead viewers and readers away from the play's
real merits and meaning. But an audience ought to be informed by the

essays about drama and tragedy that Miller has written at different stages of his career. Miller may be considered the quintessential American playwright. His emphasis on the common man embraces the metaphysics of democracy espoused by Thomas Jefferson, Walt Whitman, Ralph Waldo Emerson, and Henry David Thoreau. Whether there is such a thing as "the common man" in reality is unimportant. It is a principled man's commitment to the principles of democracy that *is* important. The principle keeps the hope and the possibility alive.

Even as Miller points out the places where America and its dream have gone wrong in *All My Sons, Death of a Salesman,* and *The Crucible,* it is the constructive criticism of the dream that keeps the faith in the American dream alive. If Miller notes in *The Crucible* and elsewhere that Americans can be greedy and excessive in their pursuit of their dreams, it must be said that only constructive criticism can keep any entity vital. Eugene O'Neill is the father of American drama because it was he who "inherited a theater tradition that was principally a frame for gaslighted frivolities. By the time he got through with it, the U. S. stage had become electric, and had learned to accommodate native-grown murder, madness, alcoholism, dark sexuality and the howling tensions of family life."[6]

For all the presence and power of O'Neill's plays, Miller is a deserving heir apparent. It is no small irony that *The Crucible* premiered in the same year that O'Neill died: America lost one great voice as another confirmed its earlier promise. It is only proper that Miller is the most American of playwrights. He directs his eyes to the Salem, Massachusetts, of 1692 and the Puritans by whom the seeds of the American dream were sown on this continent. Of them, these Puritans, Miller has summarized both the value and the dilemma and pointed out why they remain important at the end of the twentieth century: "They believed, in short, that they held in their steady hands the candle that would light the world. We have inherited this belief, and it has helped and hurt us" (5).

Two hundred years after Columbus is said to have discovered America, this continent endured its most celebrated Walpurgisnacht and two hundred and sixty years after that, America's premier social playwright, using broad brush and fine scalpel, raised for us recurrent questions that must be dealt with, and are, in this most American of plays.

The Chautauqua Opera's production of Robert Ward's opera *The Crucible* with Kathleen Fogarty (without cap) as Abigail and Kenneth Shaw (far right) as Proctor.

Photo by Thomas Montante. Courtesy of the Chautauquan Daily and by permission of the Chautauqua Opera.

13

Analogues

Verily, words can be made to fit all fancies. 'Twere safer to
be mute—

—Mary E. Wilkins, *Giles Corey, Yeoman*

Literary and artistic analogues, revisions, and versions in other media
can be helpful sources for the serious student of a particular work of
art. A great deal can be learned by noting what each artist chose from a
body of available material for inclusion in his or her own work and
how the emphasis is different or alike, how a nuance is treated (or
ignored), what is deleted, and what is submerged. So we find in literary analogues to *The Crucible* yet other paths that may be suggestive to
approach Miller's play.

The Salem witch-hunts and the events that occurred in that New
England village have held a fascination for many other writers besides
Miller. Historians, theologians, clergy, psychologists, and essayists
have, of course, expended much ink, from quill pen to word proces-
sor, on the topic. The subject has also been treated by creative writers
as disparate as Nathaniel Hawthorne and Jean-Paul Sartre, and in
media as diverse as the short story, grand opera, and film.

Much of Nathaniel Hawthorne's work, including *Twice-Told Tales* (1837) and *Mosses from an Old Manse* (1846), illustrates the fact that his principal artistic and antiquarian interests were in his New England ancestors. (It is worth noting for our discussion that the Judge Hathorne of Miller's play is based on Hawthorne's great-great-grandfather.) Perhaps Hawthorne's most famous handling of the familiar material of a "witch-meeting" is his tale "Young Goodman Brown," first published in *New England Magazine* in April 1835. Set in Salem village, the tale depicts a place and people familiar to the audience of *The Crucible*. The dark woods around Salem Village into which Brown makes his introspective journey to examine his faith is the same forest in which Abigail, Betty, and the other girls dance. One of the principal people in Hawthorne's tale is Goody Cloyse, or Sarah Cloyse, a sister of Rebecca Nurse; Cloyse was, we recall, one of the women called out by the afflicted girls, examined along with the Proctors on 11 April and executed on 19 July 1692. Historically, she had come to the startled attention of the accusing girls because, as it appeared that Rebecca Nurse would be found guilty, Cloyse stormed from the meetinghouse and amazed everyone by slamming the door behind her. "Young Goodman Brown" also contains a brief appearance by Martha Carrier, who is characterized in Hawthorne's tale as having received the devil's promise that she would be the queen of hell; Carrier was one of those found guilty, condemned to death, and hanged along with John Procter on 19 August 1692.

Yet the central point of Hawthorne's tale of Goodman Brown—indeed, one of Hawthorne's pervasive themes generally—is the psychological (rather than theological) effects of sin. Brown, like so many of Hawthorne's isolated heroes, serves as a lesson against the dangers of excessive introspection. The very self-awareness that attracted Miller to his subject is, in its process and excesses, cautioned against by Hawthorne. By the mid-nineteenth century, much of America, along with Hawthorne, seems to have reacted against the typically Puritan concept of the natural depravity of man.

Of the characters in *The Crucible*, Abigail Williams is most like Hawthorne's Goodman Brown. Hawthorne's character, like Abby, believes that all the members of the community of Salem village—reputable and pious people, elders of the church, chaste dames and dewy virgins—are given over to filthy vice and dissolute lives. Like Abigail, Brown sees the decent behavior of the men and women of Salem as pretense. The witches' sabbath presented in the tale depicts a vision of the whole earth as one stain of guilt. As this suspicion will motivate the cynical Abby, it will drive Goodman Brown to a darkly meditative, distrustful, and desperate life; he will know gloom even to his dying hour.

Hawthorne's prime lesson, illustrated by Goodman Brown, Parson Hooper of "The Minister's Black Veil" (1836), and the eponymous Ethan Brand (1850), was aimed at the kind of thinking that separates a man from the cheerful brotherhood of his fellows and a good woman's love. The unforgivable sin, Hawthorne believed, is not to be found in witchcraft but in that which inhibits or retards the natural development and growth of a human being. In that, Arthur Miller would concur.

The American short story was not the only medium to be utilized in examining the Salem witchcraft phenomenon of 1692. Nor was the examination to be confined to American writers. *Les Sorcières de Salem* is Jean-Paul Sartre's film version of *The Crucible*. This 1957 motion picture was directed by Raymond Rouleau and starred Yves Montand as John Proctor and Simone Signoret as Elizabeth. It would be beyond the purposes of this volume to pursue a complete explication at this time since the text is in French and the film, although released here in 1958, is not readily available in the United States.

Rather more to the point would be a consideration of three versions of the material that have appeared in the dramatic genre; the plays *Giles Corey of the Salem Farms* (1868) by Henry Wadsworth Longfellow, and *Giles Corey, Yeoman* (1893) by Mary E. Wilkins; and the opera *The Crucible* (1961) by Robert Ward, with a libretto by Bernard Stambler. All three texts are readily available.

Two famous American authors have created dramas on the same subject as Miller's *The Crucible,* and as might be expected, and desired, they are all three quite different plays. The nineteenth century seemed more interested in the Coreys, Giles and Martha, than in the Proctors. It was the disposition and genius of Arthur Miller that would unlock the drama of John and Elizabeth Proctor.

Henry Wadsworth Longfellow (1807–82), whose popularity as a poet was immense and brought international fame to Paul Revere's ride, the courtship of Miles Standish, Hiawatha and Minnehaha, Evangeline, and the village blacksmith, had a more vast and loyal audience than perhaps any other American poet of his time. Longfellow, a Bowdoin College classmate of Nathaniel Hawthorne, wrote a play in verse about the Salem events, *Giles Corey of the Salem Farms,* but the drama is not even mentioned in most histories of American literature or biographical sketches of the poet.[1] To suggest that the play has been neglected because it is both bad verse and bad drama is to be ungenerous. If the drama is at times disjointed, Longfellow's *Giles Corey* is not without its comparative interest.

Longfellow's composition is similar to Miller's play in a number of ways, especially in its overview of witchcraft. Eighty-five years before *The Crucible,* Longfellow provides his play with a lengthy prologue in heroic couplets that characterizes what happened "in the quiet town of Salem" (101) as "Delusions" (101)—the very first word of the prologue—and "common madness" (102). A two-point scene early in the play between Corey and his wife, Martha, recounts a conversation with Goodwife Proctor in which it is discovered that Bridget Bishop has been cried out, but, for her part, Martha Corey does "not believe / In Witches nor in Witchcraft" (121); her husband, however, does. In this play, Martha represents in her disbelief a danger to the status quo depicted by Justice John Hathorne, the magistrate, who does "not fear excess of zeal" (111) and Cotton Mather, the celebrated minister who is "a man of books and meditation" (111). Between the two lies the confirmation of the belief in "the two worlds—the seen and the unseen" (107).

Longfellow's presentation of the relationship between Giles Corey and John Proctor is brief, but it is similar in substance to Miller's if more specific in treatment. When told by another farmer that Proctor is angry with him, Corey responds, "Why does he seek to fix a quarrel on me?" (127). While this is consistent with the complex character of the relationship between Proctor and Corey in Miller's play, Longfellow is more particularly specific as to the cause of the dispute between the men. Proctor suspects that Corey has burned his house, to which Corey responds, "I burn his house? / If he says that, John Proctor is a liar! / The night his house was burned I was in bed, / And I can prove it! Why, we are old friends!" (128). Yet, consistent with his later portrayal by Miller, Corey is a volatile and violent man who goes beyond what Miller will allow him when he exclaims, "I say if Satan ever entered a man / He's in John Proctor!" (130).

More like Miller's Proctor is Longfellow's Martha Corey, who sees

> The Magistrates are blind, the people mad!
> If they would only seize the Afflicted Children,
> And put them in the Workhouse, where they should be,
> There'd be an end of all this wickedness.
>
> (139)

Martha's diagnosis and proposal for remedy are consistent with the temper of Miller's John Proctor. Moreover, Martha later tells two deacons of the church: "I do not believe / In any Witchcraft. It is a delusion" (143). Like Proctor in *The Crucible,* Martha Corey here is the voice of reason and common sense. She descries the "Afflicted Children" as "cunning, crafty girls!" (144) and proclaims them to all as such. Unwilling to play by the rules of the formal social structure, she also, like Miller's Proctor, challenges the validity of the game itself; she, of course, is tried, sentenced, and executed.

Corey himself, when accused, will not plead. Like Reverend John Hale in *The Crucible,* Richard Gardner, a sea captain and friend of Corey, visits him in prison to plead with Corey to "confess and live" (175). But Corey will not confess to a lie. Martha's example has taught him how to live, and how to die:

> As for my wife, my Martha and my Martyr,—
> . . . taught me how to live by her example,
> By her example teaches me to die,
> And leads me onward to the better life!
>
> (177)

In *The Crucible,* Giles Corey himself, along with Rebecca Nurse, will serve to teach John Proctor how to die.

Of equal interest are the contrasts between the two plays. If not all the variants are of major significance, some are interesting as curiosities. The little doll with a needle stuck into it, which plays a part in the suspicion cast on Elizabeth in act 2 of Miller's play, also turns up in Longfellow's version, but it is Bridget Bishop who is convicted on the evidence "hidden in her cellar wall / Those poppets made of rags, with headless pins / Stuck into them" (142). Likewise, there is the "yellow bird" in act 3 of *The Crucible,* which in Longfellow's fourth act "sits up there / Upon the rafters" (162). In Longfellow's meeting-house scene, the yellow bird appears to Mary Walcot. Longfellow found nothing especially notable in Abigail Williams and does not include her in his dramatis personae. Interestingly, Miller's and Longfellow's plays have several gender roles reversed. Longfellow's most admirable character, given the lengthiest speeches and most sensible position, is Martha Corey, and, lacking an Abigail, his villain is John Gloyd, Corey's hired man. Gloyd is a resentful, vexed, and envious person who, like Martha Corey and the enlightened characters in *The Crucible,* does not truly believe in the reality of the accusations of the afflicted girls. Gloyd testifies against Corey but his motives are more mundane, rooted in the ground of the land they work. With the gender roles reversed, Martha Corey, like Proctor in Miller's drama, is the voice of reason, and Gloyd, like Abigail, is the one who exacerbates the trouble. And Martha's 1868 line: "Can the innocent be guilty?" (163) will be stood on its head by the more skillful dramatist in 1953: "Why do you never wonder if Parris be innocent, or Abigail? Is the accuser always holy now?" (77).

While hero and villain are reversed as to gender in the two plays, there is no suggestion of sex or sexuality in the Longfellow. Like *The Crucible,* however, *Giles Corey* touches the theme of the possession of property. In this vein, Martha's lengthy speech (145–47) of 57 uninterrupted lines is significant because she means to illustrate the fact that the crying out is either "delusion, or it is deceit" (145) by telling the biblical story of Ahab and Naboth, demonstrating Ahab's obsession with "Naboth's vineyard, and to take / Possession of it" (146). Martha concludes her story by making her point about those who would "bear false witness / And swear away the lives of innocent people" (147) in their greed for land. While there is no sexuality, latent or otherwise in the play, Longfellow does here touch the physiocratic theme of possession of property as a motive force in human behavior. There may be no sex or sexual guilt, but the land and ownership of it becomes its own kind of lust.

Martha Corey is more clear-eyed and levelheaded than her husband, who, in Longfellow's hands, is a bit paranoid, a touch suicidal, and more superstitious than Miller's Corey. Martha sees the delusions and madness, as does Miller's Proctor, and by her example teaches her husband how to die, as Rebecca Nurse and Giles Corey provide necessary examples for Proctor in Miller's play, but there is no denying that Miller's Corey is a better dramatic creation.

Longfellow's play ends with a two-point scene in which Hathorne points "the fate / Of those who deal in Witchcrafts" (178); it is Cotton Mather who, in his response, speaks the play's last words, which characterize Corey as a victim and a martyr. Herein lies the principal distinction between the plays. Corey in Longfellow is a victim; Proctor in Miller's *The Crucible* is not.

Twenty-five years after the publication of Longfellow's drama, still another celebrated New England writer assayed a play on the same topic. It seems natural that Mary E. Wilkins (1852–1930), who would become Mary E. Wilkins Freeman after her marriage in 1902, should turn eventually to the events of the 1692 witchcraft episodes, since she was born and bred in Randolph, Massachusetts, not 30 miles south of Salem. What did not seem natural, given that her métier was the short story, was the genre she chose. When her family's fortunes declined, she had to write to earn a living, and she rapidly became a successful producer of periodical literature. Her best subject has been characterized as the decline of New England, and her stories are generally character studies filled with psychological insight. Her most renowned and best work is contained in the collections *A Humble Romance and Other Stories,* published in 1887, and *A New England Nun and Other Stories,* published in 1891. Yet in 1893, at the peak of her powers, she published her only play, *Giles Corey, Yeoman.*[2] It was not a success.

As was the case in Longfellow's play, it is Martha Corey who is the most likable and admirable character in Wilkin's drama, and she is given the play's lengthiest speeches. Like Miller's John Proctor, Wilkins's Martha Corey does not take witches and witchcraft seriously, and therefore underestimates the power of the hysteria surrounding them. An audience identifies with both characters because theirs is the reaction of intelligent, aware citizens who are vulnerable precisely because they initially cannot imagine their community taking such patent nonsense seriously.

Further, Wilkins's play is interesting to readers of *The Crucible* because Wilkins places the elements of witchcraft hysteria against a background of 1692 Salem's normal sexual rites, courtship rituals, and sexual jealousy through the story of Ann Hutchins, Paul Bayley, and Corey's daughter Olive.

Paul is a serious suitor of Olive. To please Olive, he has bought a piece of land near her mother, and he's planning with her what their house and garden will be like. He pursues her favors ardently, but, like the good girl she is, she is determined to "save them" (22) for him in marriage. While the picture here is of normal, healthy sexuality framed in coyness and youthful banter, the curtain falls on the play's first scene with Paul's reminder to Olive—and the audience—to beware the "witchcraft folly" (23). But Martha Corey, Olive's mother, spends a good deal of act 1 laughing at the notion of witches and witchcraft, while the old servant Nancy Fox (this play's version of Tituba) and Phoebe Morse, the little orphan girl who lives with the Coreys, play at witchcraft at midnight. It will be Nancy who will invoke the "yellow bird" (27) and Phoebe who will, in child's play, place the pins in the large rag doll (24–25) that will later turn up as evidence in the Salem Village meeting-house.

While the "yellow bird" and the pinned poppet are used as near comic relief in *Giles Corey, Yeoman,* John Hathorne and Minister Parris are portrayed in a manner consistent with their portrayal in *The Crucible,* and this Hathorne is, as well, like Longfellow's. (Parris does not appear in Longfellow's play.) Mary Wilkins's Hathorne is a hanging judge whose raison d'être is "we must hang, hang, hang, till we overcome!" (30).

In Wilkins's play, it is Ann Hutchins who is "afflicted"; the twist here is that Ann is laid low by sexual jealousy. Ann's mother accuses Olive of jealousy and charges Olive's mother, Martha Corey, with practicing the "devilish arts." Even Olive's kindnesses and generosity are misrepresented. In friendship, she has given Ann a cape, which now is presented as evidence against Olive. Ann is "grievously tormented" (35), not by dark arts and witches, the audience understands, but by her unacknowledged sexual jealousy of Olive's relationship with Paul Bayley. Giles Corey then enters and complicates matters by his offhand comments about his wife, which will provide Hathorne and Parris with what they take to be corroborating evidence against Martha.

Act 3 is set, like Miller's third act, in the meetinghouse in Salem Village, and the act makes it evident that Martha Corey is dangerous to Hathorne and Parris not only because she denies *she* is a witch but because she asserts, "there is no such thing as a witch" (45). Thus, like Elizabeth and John Proctor in Miller's play, she must be eliminated because her disbelief challenges the entire religious, social, and political structure and the economic system dependent upon them. In a time that posits a dualistic universe, such a denial creates a situation and a world that has no need for Hathorne or Parris, who hang people to protect their own positions, power, and illusions.

As Martha Corey sensibly points out that the problem resides within the "afflicted girls," the girls—like Abigail in *The Crucible*—create the "yellow bird" out of thin air as a diversion (46). And, as Abby in *The Crucible* will not initially implicate Proctor, whom she desires, so Ann Hutchins will not implicate Paul Bayley—"but not Paul, for he never would sign the book" (49). Mercy Lewis here, like Mercy Lewis in Miller's play, gives testimony in support of the accusations (49).

The court is not without its sanity. Jonathan Corwin is the other magistrate along with Hathorne, and he is a voice of reasonable common sense. Martha Corey gives a rational and intelligent, yet understanding, speech which runs three pages (56–58) in her own defense. A short time later Wilkins provides Martha with another sympathetic speech (65–68) in which she is assertive in her defense of her daughter Olive. Martha is admirably aggressive in her handling of the "afflicted girls," to whom she addresses reminders of their being playmates and friends of her daughter since childhood. If she is deferential to the court and proper in her manner before the justices, she is *not* intimidated by it or them. She sees it all as "sickness" and "madness," and she knows the time will come when the hysteria "shall have passed over, and all is quiet again" (67). She perceives that the girls "are in truth young, and your minds . . . sore bewildered!" (67). Moved by the speech, even Mercy Lewis, who knows that Ann Hutchins's "affliction" is, in fact, sexual jealousy (69), threatens that if Ann does not relent, she (Mercy) "will confess to the magistrates" (69). Corwin, also moved, has no fear of the supposedly cursed cape and puts it on his own shoulders. When nothing happens to him, the magistrates and Minister Parris free Olive Corey; however, they put Martha, who remains a threat, in jail. At this point, Giles Corey, who will be famous in history for *not* speaking, is given a two-page speech (70–72) in which he calls Parris a "lying devil's tool of a parson" (71) and promises to save Martha. He denounces the girls as "lying hussies . . . ill-favored little jades, puling because no man will have ye" (72), and they feign affliction until Corey is led away in chains, taken into custody by the marshal and constables. Unlike Miller's play, Corey addresses all the "afflicted girls" and lumps them together as a unit. The only two who are singled out are Mercy Lewis and Ann Hutchins, whose motive *is*, after all, sexual jealousy. While Longfellow neglects the theme of mischanneled sexuality and emphasizes property and the ownership of land, Mary Wilkins anticipates *The Crucible*'s inclusion of both motifs.

In a conversation between Paul and Olive in act 4, Paul speculates as to why Corey will stand mute at his trial (81). The movement toward the second thematic consideration of the play, the ownership of the land, is accelerated and becomes more prominent when it is disclosed that Olive's half-sisters and their husbands have sent written testimony against their father, Giles Corey. Olive believes that she is in part responsible for what has befallen her parents (82), and the brief act concludes with the announcement that Paul will go to Boston to appeal to the governor.

Giles Corey's cell in Salem jail is the setting for act 5. Giles is heavily chained. It is six weeks later, and a month has passed since his wife Martha has "died on Gallows Hill" (85). With Martha gone, the play is left to Corey, and Wilkins's creation displays the same strength, sardonic wit, and sense of humor that will characterize Miller's portrait of Corey. Bayley, it is disclosed, has failed to move Governor Phipps. This comes as no surprise, for Corey sees the "whole land is now a bedlam, and the Governors and the magistrates swell the ravings" (88).

Corey insists that Paul marry Olive "within three weeks" (88); he will deed all his property to Paul when he marries Olive. While some of this may offend a contemporary feminist reader, Wilkins's Corey believed that it is "ever a hard world . . . hard enough for a man; a young maid must needs have somebody to hold aside the boughs for her" in a land and time "not cleared any more than the woods of Massachusetts" (89). Surely the liberated reader of today can forgive this 1893 portrayal of fatherly concern in 1692, especially since it is balanced by Wilkin's portrayal of an independent, intelligent, and assertive Martha. In Wilkins's version, Corey will stand mute at his trial so that, while he says he bears no ill will to his sons-in-law and daughters, his last will and testament will stand as a "good and trusty document" (90). While Wilkins's Giles Corey does not accuse Putnam, as Miller's does, he makes his decision to stand mute with a practical eye to the ownership of the land. Thus in Wilkins's play, Corey is moved to stand mute by economic matters and the physiocratic ideals upon which this nation was, in part, founded. This economic theory, manifest here—that the land and its products are the only true wealth—is a touchstone for many of America's founding citizens. Miller's play, seen in the reflected light of Wilkins's drama, presents an accurate historical picture of beliefs and values at the end of the seventeenth century on this continent in the incubational period of the American dream. If *The Crucible* takes some liberties with facts and dates, it is true to the essence of its subject.

Arthur Miller's and Mary E. Wilkins's Giles Corey will undergo being pressed beneath stone weights until his death not because he is possessive or greedy and certainly not because of acquisitiveness, but because of the principle that security of person and property are essential to an individual's well-being. Seen in this context, Miller's Proctor becomes even more heroic because his decision to go to his own death is based upon principles even more inspired and transcendent. Martha Corey spoke like "a martyr" at her death; Giles Corey goes to his death a recalcitrant mute; Miller's Proctor may be seen, as human and practical as he is depicted, to represent more timeless spiritual values.

Yet there is that something in Wilkins's Corey that steps beyond the utilitarian. He makes it clear that he is *not* dying just so his property goes to Olive. Of his motivation, he adds, "the goods be the least of it" (94). He believes that by his death "the backbone of this great evil in the land shall be broke by the same weight" (94). The third and final element in his complex motivation is "to make amends to Martha" (95). Like Miller's Proctor, Corey recognizes his part in what has happened to his wife, but unlike Proctor, he does not accept responsibility for the larger catastrophe.

Nevertheless, a last temptation does come to Corey. His daughter comes to beg him "to plead at your trial" (97) that he "may yet be acquitted" (97). Miller's Proctor declines confession for noble reasons, but when Wilkins's Corey dismisses his daughter, it is with the words, "womenkind should meddle not with men's plans" (97). Corey's motivation suffers in comparison to the expansive growth and understanding in Miller's protagonist. In the 1953 play, Proctor spends his final moments in powerful growth of person. Wilkins offers a quietly moving but melodramatic domestic tableau of a weeping Olive stitching the seams in Corey's coat so he can "look tidy at the trial" (98) for his wife's sake.

Act 6 takes its reader three weeks later in time to a three-point scene in which Corwin, Hathorne, and Parris describe the violence of Corey's death, which occurs offstage, and the subsequent conversation suggests to an audience that the rule of reason has begun to arrive (101). This final act concludes with the news that Corey is dead and he has not spoken. Olive and Paul appear, she in a white gown and white bonnet (102). The fact that it is their wedding day as well as the day of Corey's death is meant to suggest to the audience the bittersweet realization that "we be far set in that course of nature . . . with the apple blossoms and the rose-buds, where the beginning cannot be without the end" (104), a familiar theme in world literature.

More relevant, however, is the indication that it is Corey's "dumb-ness" and his death that will "save the colonies" and "put an end to this dreadful madness" (106). The afflicted girls and the magistrates and ministers evaporate from importance to the play, and the Proctors are never mentioned. But Wilkins's play, with its emphases on the domestic elements and the colonial physiocratic ideals that will grow into such a large part of the American dream, is a nice contrast against which to view *The Crucible*.

Miller's play, coming 60 years after Wilkins's drama, points to both the corruption of the hopes and ideals of late-nineteenth-century America and the seeds of that corruption planted in the American psyche by the colonial Puritans. The moral rectitude and ethical certainty noted by Miller helped to both sustain and undermine the American dream; the discipline, dedication, devotion, and direction that allowed the Puritans to survive past the horror of 1692 permitted a nation to achieve ideological and pragmatic world leadership. Mary E. Wilkins's world would not have allowed for the perception or presentation of the dichotomy explicit in this vision; Arthur Miller's world does.

Sometimes in the attempt to define what something is, it is prof-itable to indicate what it is *not*. There are, therefore, things to be sug-gested by looking back at *The Crucible* from the perspective of the 1961 opera version of it, with libretto by Bernard Stambler and music by Robert Ward.[3] The opera was commissioned by the New York City Opera under a grant from the Ford Foundation and had its first per-formance 26 October 1961.

The opera enhances several elements of the play by bringing them more clearly into the foreground, while other things become sug-gestive or curious by their deletion. Two examples serve for the moment as illustrations. At the conclusion of a meeting in the misty moonlit woods, Abigail's parting words to John in Stambler's libretto are "but if your snivelling Elizabeth dies—remember, remember, it is you who kill her" (20). This changes things. Proctor's subsequent actions can be construed as a test of wills with Abigail. It could be interpreted that Proctor acts to prove Abby wrong. It becomes, then, for Proctor an avoidance of another sort of, or degree of, guilt—the responsibility for Elizabeth's death. This is not an issue in Miller's play because Elizabeth is pregnant, as she is *not* in the opera.

There are minor changes in character that are of no readily apparent significance. So, for example, it is Marshal Herrick who is the nearly drunken turnkey in the opening of Miller's act 4, while Cheever is the besotted functionary lurching about carrying a bottle at the same moment in the opera. Of more import is the change in character of Danforth. In the opera's third act, Danforth is moved to "press" Giles Corey in a fit of rage at Corey's physical altercation with Putnam. The Danforth of the opera is less the man of "some humor and sophistication" (85) of Miller's play and more a violent, forceful martinet who acts "sadistically" (22).

When Miller first considered using the witch trials of 1692 as the subject of a play, it did occur to him almost immediately that the material by its very nature was operatic. And in production, the opera is an artistic triumph. The music by Robert Ward is fully deserving of its 1962 Pulitzer Prize, for the score serves the libretto by Bernard Stambler—and, for the most part, Miller's intentions—remarkably well. The music is subtle—often nearly sublime; often, in appropriate moments, quite powerful—and it enhances the varying moods and tones of the drama's progress. There are no grand opera set pieces of the length one might find in Puccini or Verdi, but elements of Ward's score can insinuate themselves into and punctuate an important detail not noted previously. The music is always the handmaiden to the text, and is of a distinctly American cast, with echoes of George Gershwin and Aaron Copland. The use of identifiably American nuances in the music is especially appropriate for this work: Americans historically have believed that there are things worth dying for, and that is, of course, one of *The Crucible*'s major themes. If the opera is not as well known or lyrical as *Porgy and Bess* (1935), it belongs on the same top shelf with it.

There are, of course, important differences between the opera and its predecessor. In Ward's opera, there is no meeting between Proctor and Abigail in the initial act. Because of the varied nature of the *genre*, the audience sees Abby's reactions "as she becomes increasingly ecstatic" (14) as she hears the sound of Proctor's voice, even though she remains upstairs in Betty's bedroom as Proctor enters Parris's parlor below.

Much of the opera is, of necessity, more compressed, compact, and concentrated in the interest of time. The rag poppet in the opera's third act must be already set on the fireplace mantle in the Proctor home and not carried on by Mary Warren and presented to Elizabeth as it is in the play. Often, depth of characterization and some sense of irony is lost. Miller's second act is much truncated and scenes compressed. The full development of Proctor's relationship with and opinion of Parris and Parris's conduct as a minister is lost, and the entire scene in which Proctor must recite the commandments, neglecting to mention adultery, is deleted. There is far less development of Hale's character and his relationship with the Proctors because in Ward's work Hale is never alone with them, since Cheever, whose character is much more fully developed than in Miller's play, arrives at the Proctor home with him. On the other hand, the significance of the drama's last line, which can be lost on the viewer of the play, becomes more suggestive in the opera, since the music that accompanies, supports, and carries the line is similar to that which accompanies Proctor's line to Elizabeth in the opera's second act: "look you sometimes for the goodness in me" (16). The repetition of the phrase of music reminds the audience of the earlier occasion, and Elizabeth's final words bring the audience instantly back to the earlier domestic scene and the pastoral orchestral prelude that precedes it, and is moved by the echoing "he have his goodness now" (32). An audience that might have overlooked the significance of the line's repetition in the play will not do so in the opera.

Quite a significant revision in the opera is that Abigail appears in Proctor's cell at the drama's penultimate moment to offer him money, clothes, freedom, and easily achieved escape with her. This addition enriches the dilemma with which Proctor must deal; the depth and complexity of his character are made manifest as the audience sees, and hears, Proctor's rejection of one final temptation of the flesh.

The most notable revision is that the opera restores the celebrated meeting in the woods between Proctor and Abigail (the act 2, scene 2 that Miller deleted from the play). Ward and Stambler restore it as act 3, scene 1. Far from suggesting the madness apparent in Abigail in the original deleted scene, the scene in the opera is supported by lush, romantic music, the most memorable music in the opera. Quite different than the Abigail of the play's deleted scene, she appears here openly suggestive and quite erotic, attempting to lure John back to her "like some great stallion wildly pantin for me" (20). The audience experiences a scene quite different in characterization—highly charged and overtly sexual. Abigail denounces the "psalm-singing hypocrites" (20) of the Salem community while Proctor, struggling with base instincts, sees her call for "Holy work" as "fraud, pretense and fraud" (20). Significantly, he speaks the word that she uses in the play—*pretense.* While he sees pretense in her actions, she sees it in the people of Salem specifically and in human nature generally. The restoration of this scene and Abigail's appearance in the opera's final act to offer Proctor escape prompts the reader to reconsider their relationship.

The search for the significance of these revisions leads eventually to the genesis of the opera. The credits for Ward's *The Crucible* are quite specific: "based on the play by Arthur Miller." When Robert Ward initially conceived of the project, he wanted to know if Miller would consider doing the libretto.[4] Miller and Ward had one meeting. Miller wanted no involvement with the composition of the libretto; Ward recalls that Miller wasn't sure he knew what should go into it, and also that he was working on the screenplay for *The Misfits* at that time.[5] Since then, of course, Miller did provide the book and lyrics for *Up From Paradise* in 1974, a musical version of his *The Creation of the World and Other Business.* Subsequent to Ward's meeting with Miller, Ward and Stambler had a half-dozen meetings with the playwright. Ward remembers that Miller's main concerns were for the characters, that they remain essentially the same and that Ward and Stambler not disturb the intention of the play. The opera is, for the most part, quite true to Miller's text, and if Proctor does *not* sign the confession in Stambler's libretto, for example, he is often given stage business to do so in production, and, in any case, it is a matter of dramatic compression that does not violate Miller's intention—at least not to any great degree.

As for the major revisions, Ward is direct and forthcoming. Regarding Elizabeth's not being pregnant in the opera, Ward says it is "one of those elements in the play that had to be deleted because of considerations of time. We did think a lot about it, but when you get to the hierarchy of those things to be cut, it either had to be more fully developed or deleted."[6] It was deleted even though Ward knew the pregnancy is historically accurate and vital to the fact that Elizabeth is permitted to live both in history and in Miller's play. Members of the opera's audience who have been following carefully are left with the question unresolved as to why this Elizabeth is not hanged.

The restoration of the scene in the woods is a larger matter, and it was Ward's doing. That the scene is added to the opera at all is due to both Ward's own genius and serendipity. Stambler and Ward had seen the Manhattan Theatre Club revival of the play, which included the scene. When he sought the text of the play, however, Ward could not find a published text with the scene in print. He then asked Miller about it, and the playwright replied, "Oh, that scene; forget it. It's no good."[7] For the scene in the woods, Ward wanted to use music and material he had already written and removed from the first act. Miller finally acceded to the resurrection of the moonlit outdoor scene since it had already been completely scored. "Erotic" is Ward's own choice of word to describe the music in the restored scene, and it is the apposite term. Had Ward known that the scene had been deleted from the play, he might not have composed the music at all.

Much earlier, before Ward and Stambler had undertaken the project, Aaron Copland had been approached to do the opera but declined. Ward spoke with Copland, who didn't think *he* should compose the opera and wasn't sure he could do the last act. Ward's final act provides a solemn opening with Tituba and Sarah Good. This was provided for two reasons—one mundane, another artistic. Ward and Stambler felt that they wanted to give the performer who sang the role of Tituba "another turn," and at the same time believed that musically "the despair and disintegration of the entire community is in that final act."[8] The two individual women serve as a synecdoche for the whole of Salem.

Likewise, Ward and Stambler have Abigail return in act 4 because "it's too long for her to be off. The audience wants to see her again."[9] While this seems at wide variance with Miller's intention, Ward handles it well. Early in the final act, Abigail presents Proctor with an ultimate temptation of the flesh, one that is almost surreal in character, as though it is in the workings of Proctor's subconscious. When he dismisses her, the action enhances Proctor's heroism, but Abigail is rid of early so the remainder of the last act can focus on John and Elizabeth, which is Ward's intention, and finally on Proctor alone.

It is certain, and it cannot be pretended otherwise, that Ward's opera cannot properly be considered an analogue. Robert Ward's music and Bernard Stambler's libretto provide a supercharged version of the play, using much of Miller's text verbatim. And they are for the most part true to Miller's intention, allowing for the exceptions noted above. In fact, the last line of the opera is exactly as Miller has it when Elizabeth declares, "He have his goodness now. God forbid I take it from him!" (145).

In Longfellow's play about the Salem farmer and his wife falsely condemned for sorcery, there is no hint of sex or sexual guilt; in the drama by Wilkins, there is evidence of normal courtship rituals and a vital sexual undercurrent. In Ward's opera, the sensuality and sexuality of Miller's play have become overtly erotic. From 1868 to 1893, from 1953 to 1961, each work reflects not only the writers but what is permissible and acceptable in each age.

Still Miller's play has an indefatigable life of its own. Yet another Broadway revival of *The Crucible* has already been performed by Tony Randall's National Actors Theatre, starring Martin Sheen. It opened on 8 November 1991 and ran until 5 January 1992 at the Belasco Theatre, separated by only three city blocks but almost four decades from its initial debut.[10]

Has *The Crucible* stood the test of time? It has endured for these first 40 years. What is to come in another 40 or 400 years no one can know. It may be, however, that more people do indeed know this play than remember Senator Joseph McCarthy, McCarthyism, and the witch-hunts of the 1950s; more than that come to their first knowledge of the Salem witchcraft trials through the play. Theatrical and literary tastes may change, and what is accepted may change, but it may be a long stay for those who wait for the theatrical and literary lights to dim on *The Crucible*.

Notes and References

Chapter 1

1. George Lincoln Burr, ed., *Narratives of the Witchcraft Cases 1648–1706* (New York: Scribner's Sons, 1914), 361; hereafter cited in text.

2. The theory that Corey chose the "piene forte et dure" in order to preserve his right to bequeath his property and thus avoid what had happened to Procter's property has been questioned.

3. Arthur Miller, *Timebends: A Life* (New York: Grove Press, 1987), 334; hereafter cited in text as *Timebends*.

Chapter 2

1. James J. Martine, "'All in a Boiling Soup': An Interview with Arthur Miller," in *Critical Essays on Arthur Miller,* ed. James J. Martine (Boston: G. K. Hall, 1979), 185; hereafter cited in text.

2. Arthur Miller, "Again They Drink from the Cup of Suspicion," *New York Times,* 26 November 1989, sec. 2, p. 36; hereafter cited in text as "Again They Drink."

Chapter 3

1. A. Peter Foulkes, "Arthur Miller's *The Crucible*: Contexts of Understanding and Misunderstanding," in *Theater und Drama in Amerika: Aspekte und Interpretationen,* ed. Edgar Lohner and Rudolf Haas (Berlin: Erich Schmidt Verlag, 1978), 301; reprinted in A. P. Foulkes, *Literature and Propaganda* (London: Methuen, 1983), 93.

2. Tom F. Driver, *Romantic Quest and Modern Query: A History of the Modern Theatre* (New York: Delta, 1970), 313–14.

3. See John Gassner, *The Theatre in Our Times* (New York: Crown, 1954), 367, for his original estimate; and *Theatre at the Crossroads* (New York: Holt, Rinehart and Winston, 1960), 274–78, for his revised evaluation.

4. Gerald Weales, Introduction to *The Crucible: Text and Criticism,* ed. Gerald Weales (New York: Viking, 1971), xvii.

5. Sheridan Morley, "The Crucible," *Playbill: The National Theatre Magazine,* 31 July 1990, 65.

Chapter 5

1. See, for example, William T. Liston, "John Proctor's Playing in *The Crucible*," *Midwest Quarterly* 20 (1979); 394.

Chapter 6

1. Lajos Egri, *The Art of Dramatic Writing* (New York: Simon and Schuster, 1960), 165.

2. Brooks Atkinson, "Arthur Miller's *The Crucible* in a New Edition with Several New Actors and One New Scene," *New York Times,* 2 July 1953, 20; reprinted in Weales, 194–96.

Chapter 8

1. John Gassner, "Miller's *The Crucible* as Event and Play," in *Twentieth Century Interpretations of "The Crucible,"* ed. John H. Ferres (Englewood Cliffs: Prentice Hall, 1972), 30.

2. Arthur Miller, Introduction to *A View from the Bridge* (New York: Viking, 1960), viii; hereafter cited in text as *View*.

Chapter 9

1. See, for example, Chadwick Hansen, *Witchcraft at Salem* (New York: Braziller, 1969), 31; Samuel G. Drake, *Annals of Witchcraft in New England* (New York: Benjamin Blom, 1967), 189; and Burr, 153.

2. William J. McGill, Jr., "The Crucible of History: Arthur Miller's John Proctor," *New England Quarterly* 54, no. 2 (June 1981): 260. See also Paul Boyer and Stephen Nissenbaum, *Salem Possessed: The Social Origins of Witchcraft* (Cambridge: Harvard University Press, 1974), 200.

3. Carl E. Bain, *The Norton Introduction to Literature: Drama* (New York: Norton, 1973), xxiv.

4. See, for example, *Timebends,* 341.

Notes and References

Chapter 10

1. Benjamin Nelson, *Arthur Miller: Portrait of a Playwright* (New York: David McKay, 1970), 41.

Chapter 11

1. Arthur Miller, *Death of a Salesman* (New York: Penguin Books, 1976), 36–40; hereafter cited in text.

2. See, for example, Beverly Hume, "Linda Loman as 'The Woman' in Miller's *Death of a Salesman*," *Notes on Modern American Literature* 9, no. 3 (Winter 1985): 14.

Chapter 12

1. Arthur Miller, "On Recognition," *Michigan Quarterly Review* 2 (October 1963): 213–20; reprinted in *The Theater Essays of Arthur Miller,* ed. Robert A. Martin (New York: Viking, 1978), 248 (hereafter cited in text as *Essays*).

2. See, for example, Alvin Whitley, "Arthur Miller: An Attempt at Modern Tragedy," *Transactions of the Wisconsin Academy of Sciences, Arts, and Letters* 42 (1953): 257–62; Phillip Walker, "Arthur Miller's 'The Crucible': Tragedy or Allegory?" *Western Speech* 20, no. 4 (Fall 1956): 222–24; John Gassner, "Tragic Perspectives: A Sequence of Queries," *TDR* 2, no. 3 (May 1958); esp. 20–22; M. W. Steinberg, "Arthur Miller and the Idea of Modern Tragedy," *Dalhousie Review* 40 (1960): 329–40 (reprinted in *Arthur Miller: A Collection of Critical Essays,* ed. Robert W. Corrigan [Englewood Cliffs, N.J.: Prentice-Hall, 1969], 81–93; John Prudhoe, "Arthur Miller and the Tradition of Tragedy," *English Studies* 43 (1962): 430–39; Penelope Curtis, "The Crucible," *Critical Review,* 1965, no. 8:45–58 (reprinted in Weales, 255–71); Clinton W. Trowbridge, "Arthur Miller: Between Pathos and Tragedy," *Modern Drama* 10 (1967): 221–32 (reprinted in Martine, 125–35); and Neil Carson, *Arthur Miller* (New York: Grove Press, 1982), 60–76, and esp. 78–80. Especially interesting and suggestive is Alan A. Stambusky, "Arthur Miller: Aristotelian Canons in the Twentieth Century Drama," in *Modern American Drama: Essays in Criticism,* ed. William E. Taylor (DeLand, Florida: Everett/Edwards, 1968), 91–115.

3. Joseph T. Shipley, "Arthur Miller's New Melodrama Is Not What It Seems to Be," *New Leader* 36 (February 1953): 25–26 (reprinted in Weales, 201–3).

4. Otto Reinert, ed., *Classic through Modern Drama* (Boston: Little, Brown, 1970), xxviii.

5. William Flint Thrall and Addison Hibbard, *A Handbook to Literature,* revised and enlarged by C. Hugh Holman (New York: Odyssey Press, 1960), 488.

6. Paul Gray, "New Views of a Playwright's Long Journey," *Time,* 7 November 1988, 120–21.

Chapter 13

1. Henry Wadsworth Longfellow, "Giles Corey of the Salem Farms" in *The New-England Tragedies* (Boston: Ticknor and Fields, 1868), 101–79; hereafter cited in text.

2. Mary E. Wilkins, *Giles Corey, Yeoman* (New York: Harper and Brothers, 1893); hereafter cited in text.

3. Robert Ward, *The Crucible: An Opera in Four Acts,* based on the play by Arthur Miller, libretto by Bernard Stambler (New York: Highgate Press/Galaxy Music, 1961). A recording of the New York City Opera's production, which won both a New York Critics Circle Citation and the Pulitzer Prize for 1962, is available from Composers Recordings, CRI-168.

4. Robert Ward, personal interview, 5 August 1991. Ward's opera was given an outstanding production on 2 and 5 August 1991 by the Chautauqua Opera, Chautauqua, New York. Directed by Albert Takazauckas, it featured Kathleen Fogarty as Abigail, Kenneth Shaw as Proctor, and Jane Bunnell as Elizabeth. Robert Ward attended the 2 August 1991 performance. Information concerning the composition of the opera and revisions made to Miller's text is drawn from my interview with Ward, who was generous with his time and especially gracious and cooperative.

5. Ward, interview, 5 August 1991.

6. Ibid.

7. Ibid. There is no mention of Ward, Stambler, or the opera in *Timebends.*

8. Ibid.

9. Ibid.

10. "Onstage on B'way," *Playbill: The National Theatre Magazine,* 31 August 1991, 35.

Selected Bibliography

Primary Works

Plays

That They May Win. In *The Best One-Act Plays of 1944,* edited by Margaret Mayorga, 45–60. New York: Dodd, Mead, 1945.

The Man Who Had All the Luck. In *Cross-Section,* edited by Edwin Seaver, 486–552. New York: L. B. Fischer, 1944.

All My Sons. New York: Reynal and Hitchcock, 1947.

Death of a Salesman. New York: Viking, 1949. Reprint. *Death of a Salesman: Certain Private Conversations in Two Acts and a Requiem* (Special illustrated edition). New York: Viking, 1981; New York: Limited Editions Club, 1984.

An Enemy of the People. New York: Viking, 1951. Reprint. New York: Penguin, 1977. Miller's adaptation of Ibsen's play.

The Crucible. New York: Viking, 1953, 1971. Reprint. New York: Penguin, 1971, 1978. New York: Bantam, 1981.

A View from the Bridge and *A Memory of Two Mondays.* Published as *A View from the Bridge: Two One-Act Plays by Arthur Miller.* New York: Viking, 1955. One-act version of *A View from the Bridge* also in *Theatre Arts* 40, no. 9 (September 1956): 49–68.

A View from the Bridge (revised two-act version). New York: Dramatists Play Service, 1957. Reprint. New York: Compass, 1960.

Arthur Miller's Collected Plays. New York: Viking, 1957. Includes *All My Sons, Death of a Salesman, The Crucible, A Memory of Two Mondays,* and the two-act version of *A View from the Bridge.*

After the Fall. New York: Viking, 1964. Reprint. New York: Penguin, 1980.

Incident at Vichy. New York: Viking, 1965. Reprint. New York: Penguin, 1985.

The Price. New York: Viking, 1968. Reprint. New York: Penguin, 1985.

The Creation of the World and Other Business. New York: Viking, 1973.

The American Clock. New York: Viking, 1980.

Arthur Miller's Collected Plays, Volume II. New York: Viking, 1981. Includes *The Misfits, After the Fall, Incident at Vichy, The Price, The Creation of the World and Other Business,* and *Playing For Time.*

The Archbishop's Ceiling. London: Methuen, 1984; New York: Dramatist's Play Service, 1985; New York: Grove Press, 1988.

Elegy for a Lady and *Some Kind of Love Story.* Two one-act plays published as *Two-way Mirror.* New York: Dramatist's Play Service, 1982.

Up From Paradise (musical based on *The Creation of the World and Other Business*). Libretto by Arthur Miller, music by Stanley Silverman. New York: S. French, 1984.

I Can't Remember Anything and *Clara.* Two one-act plays published as *Danger: Memory!* London: Methuen, 1986; New York: Grove Press, 1986.

Books

Situation Normal. New York: Reynal and Hitchcock, 1944.

Focus. New York: Reynal and Hitchcock, 1945. Reprint. New York: Arbor House, 1984.

The Misfits (screenplay-novel). New York: Viking, 1961. Reprint. New York: Scribner, 1987.

Jane's Blanket (children's book). New York: Crowell Collier, 1963.

I Don't Need You Anymore (short-story collection). New York: Viking, 1967. Reprint. New York: Scribner, 1987.

In Russia. With Inge Morath. New York: Viking, 1969.

The Portable Arthur Miller. Edited by Harold Clurman. New York: Viking, 1971.

In the Country. With Inge Morath. New York: Viking, 1977.

Selected Bibliography

The Theater Essays of Arthur Miller. Edited by Robert A. Martin. New York: Viking, 1978.

Chinese Encounters. With Inge Morath. New York: Farrar, Straus, Giroux, 1979.

Playing for Time: A Screenplay. New York: Bantam, 1981.

Salesman in Beijing. New York: Viking, 1984.

Timebends: A Life. New York: Grove Press, 1987.

Articles and Parts of Books

"The Pussycat and the Expert Plumber Who Was a Man." In *One Hundred Non-Royalty Radio Plays,* edited by William Kozlenko, 20–30. New York: Greenberg, 1941.

"William Ireland's Confession." In *One Hundred Non-Royalty Radio Plays,* edited by William Kozlenko, 512–21. New York: Greenberg, 1941.

"Grandpa and the Statue." In *Radio Drama in Action,* edited by Erik Barnouw, 265–81. New York: Farrar and Rinehart, 1945.

"The Story of Gus." In *Radio's Best Plays,* edited by Joseph Liss, 303–19. New York: Greenberg, 1947.

"The Guardsman." In *Theatre Guild on the Air,* edited by H. William Fitelson, 69–97. New York: Rinehart, 1947. Radio adaptation of play by Ferenc Molnar.

"Three Men on a Horse." In *Theatre Guild on the Air,* edited by H. William Fitelson, 207–38. New York: Rinehart, 1947. Radio adaptation of the play by George Abbott and John C. Holm.

"Subsidized Theatre." *New York Times,* 22 June 1947, sec. 2, p. 1.

"Tragedy and the Common Man." *New York Times,* 27 February 1949, sec. 2, pp. 1, 3.

"Arthur Miller on 'The Nature of Tragedy.' " *New York Herald Tribune,* 27 March 1949, sec. 5, pp. 1, 2.

"The Family in Modern Drama." *Atlantic Monthly* 197 (April 1956): 35–41.

"The Playwright and the Atomic World." *Colorado Quarterly* 5 (Autumn 1956): 117–37.

"The Shadows of the Gods." *Harper's* 217 (August 1958): 35–43.

"Bridge to a Savage World." *Esquire* 50 (October 1958): 185–90.

"Again They Drink from the Cup of Suspicion." *New York Times,* 26 November 1989, sec. 2, pp. 5 and 36.

Secondary Sources

BOOKS

Bhatia, Santosh K. *Arthur Miller: Social Drama as Tragedy*. New York: Heinemann, 1985. Evaluates six Miller plays, including *The Crucible,* as tragedy.

Boyer, Paul, and Stephen Nissenbaum. *Salem Possessed: The Social Origins of Witchcraft*. Cambridge: Harvard University Press, 1974. A good source on the complex social causes of the historical events in Salem Village.

Burr, George Lincoln, ed. *Narratives of the Witchcraft Cases 1648–1706*. New York: Charles Scribner's Sons, 1914. Includes an account of John Procter's trial, imprisonment, and execution.

Carson, Neil. *Arthur Miller*. New York: Grove Press, 1982. Chapter on *The Crucible* (60–76) is an interesting analysis of the hysteria that affects Salem and Miller's use of it.

Corrigan, Robert W. *Arthur Miller: A Collection of Critical Essays*. Englewood Cliffs: Prentice-Hall, 1969. A nice gathering of essays edited by an outstanding scholar.

Drake, Samuel G. *Annals of Witchcraft in New England*. New York: Benjamin Blom, 1869, 1967. Includes an account of the events of 1692 (186–208).

Evans, Richard I. *Psychology and Arthur Miller*. New York: Dutton, 1969. A dialogue between Evans, a psychologist, and Miller.

Ferres, John H., ed. *Twentieth Century Interpretations of "The Crucible."* Englewood Cliffs: Prentice-Hall, 1972. Contains 20 articles and reviews.

Hansen, Chadwick. *Witchcraft at Salem*. New York: Braziller, 1969. Readable and suggestive account of events at Salem.

Hayman, Ronald. *Arthur Miller*. New York: Ungar, 1972. Individual chapters on the plays from *All My Sons* to *The Price* center on Miller's social commitment and his concern to analyze in terms of process.

Hogan, Robert. *Arthur Miller*. Pamphlets on American Writers, no. 40. Minneapolis: University of Minnesota Press, 1964. Briefly views plays up to *Incident at Vichy* and is insightful on *The Crucible;* a good introduction to the plays.

Huftel, Sheila. *Arthur Miller: The Burning Glass*. New York: Citadel, 1965. If the chapter on *The Crucible* is standard fare, most interesting is a transcript of Miller's appearance before HUAC (31–50).

Martin, Robert A., ed. *Arthur Miller: New Perspectives.* Englewood Cliffs: Prentice-Hall, 1982. A good collection edited by a topflight Miller scholar.

Martine, James J., ed. *Critical Essays on Arthur Miller.* Boston: G. K. Hall, 1979. A collection of articles, including an extensive bibliographic essay.

Moss, Leonard. *Arthur Miller, Revised Edition.* Boston: Twayne, 1980. The chapter "Four 'Social Plays'" offers a nice reading of *The Crucible* in context with *A View from the Bridge, A Memory of Two Mondays,* and *The Misfits* by a reputable Miller scholar.

Nelson, Benjamin. *Arthur Miller: Portrait of a Playwright.* New York: McKay, 1970. Remains the most thorough biographic study and best introduction to the dramatist.

Roudané, Matthew C., ed. *Conversations with Arthur Miller.* Jackson: University Press of Mississippi, 1987. A worthwhile and convenient collection of 35 of the best Miller interviews spanning from 1947 to 1986.

Schlueter, June, and James K. Flanagan. *Arthur Miller.* New York: Ungar, 1987. A nice introduction to the author's oeuvre, discussing themes and thought in 10 plays.

Starkey, Marion L. *The Devil in Massachusetts.* New York: Knopf, 1950. The book that rekindled Miller's interest in Salem, written in what he calls "remarkably well-organized detail."

Upham, Charles W. *Salem Witchcraft.* New York: Ungar, 1959. First published in 1867, this book is considered the standard history of the time. Miller used it for his research and calls it a "quiet nineteenth-century masterpiece."

Weales, Gerald, ed. *The Crucible: Text and Criticism.* New York: Viking, 1971. Contains, in addition to the text, 12 reviews, a good collection of essays, and excerpts from historical documents.

Welland, Dennis. *Arthur Miller.* New York: Grove, 1961. An early yet still worthwhile introduction to the plays.

ARTICLES AND PARTS OF BOOKS

Bentley, Eric. "The Innocence of Arthur Miller." In *What Is Theatre? Incorporating "The Dramatic Event" and Other Reviews 1944–1967.* New York: Atheneum, 1968, 62–65. Reprinted in Weales, 204–9. The most celebrated attack and most quoted review on the play and its author, claiming that liberalism and innocence reduce the play to melodrama.

Bergeron, David M. "Arthur Miller's *The Crucible* and Nathaniel Hawthorne: Some Parallels." *English Journal* 58, no. 1 (1969): 47–55. Diminishes the McCarthyism parallels and, evaluating the play on its own merits, calls it high tragedy. Compares Proctor to Hawthorne's Dimmesdale.

Bigsby, C. W. E. "Arthur Miller." In *A Critical Introduction to Twentieth-Century American Drama 2: Williams/Miller/Albee.* Cambridge: Cambridge University Press, 1984, 135–248. This in-depth examination of the dramatist's work includes a careful relating of the play to Miller's HUAC experiences and considers the play's relation to the questions of authority and the existence of evil.

Blau, Herbert. "The Whole Man and the Real Witch." In *Arthur Miller: A Collection of Critical Essays,* edited by Robert W. Corrigan, 123–130. Englewood Cliffs: Prentice-Hall, 1969. Worthwhile article on the production values of the play by a codirector of the Repertory Theatre of Lincoln Center.

Bonnet, Jean-Marie. "Society vs. the Individual in Arthur Miller's *The Crucible." English Studies* 63, no. 1 (February 1982): 32–36. Analyzes the duality in the drama, which is said to be bifocal, shifting between the conflicts within Proctor and his conflicts with society.

Budick, E. Miller. "History and Other Spectres in Arthur Miller's *The Crucible." Modern Drama* 28, no. 4 (December 1985): 535–52. Provocatively examines the demon of moral absolutism and finds that Proctor suffers as much from moral arrogance as the Salem judges. Suggests Proctor's story is the story of American Puritanism.

Ditsky, John. "Stone, Fire, and Light: Approaches to *The Crucible." North Dakota Quarterly* 46, no. 2 (1978): 65–72. Attempts to explain the play's enduring popularity; examines the play's theatricality, including setting, imagery, language, and action.

Foulkes, A. Peter. "Arthur Miller's *The Crucible:* Contexts of Understanding and Misunderstanding." In *Theater und Drama in Amerika: Aspekte und Interpretationen,* edited by Edgar Lohner and Rudolf Hass, 295–309. Berlin: Schmidt, 1978. Reviews basic McCarthyism background and reads the play as antipropaganda. With five new opening paragraphs and three new closing paragraphs, this appears verbatim as "Demystifying the Witch Hunt" in Foulkes's *Literature and Propaganda,* 83–104, 114. London: Methuen, 1983.

Hansen, Chadwick. "The Metamorphosis of Tituba, or Why American Intellectuals Can't Tell An Indian Witch from a Negro." *New England Quarterly* 47, no. 1 (1974): 3–12. Discusses the character of Tituba in literature and history.

Hughes, Catharine R. *"The Crucible."* In *Plays, Politics, and Polemics,* 15–25. New York: Drama Book Specialists, 1973. Relates the play to McCarthyism and the ambience of its setting.

Selected Bibliography

Liston, William T. "John Proctor's Playing in *The Crucible*." *Midwest Quarterly* 20 (1979): 394–403. Focuses on Proctor's use of metaphor; proposes that Proctor is a threat to the community because his is a literary mind.

Martin, Robert A. "Arthur Miller's *The Crucible*: Background and Sources." *Modern Drama* 20 (1977): 279–92. Reprinted in Martine, 93–104. An evaluation of the play's sources by a knowledgeable Miller scholar.

McGill, William J., Jr. "The Crucible of History: Arthur Miller's John Proctor." *New England Quarterly* 54, no. 2 (June 1981): 258–64. Points to significant differences between the historical Procter and Miller's protagonist, and concludes that Miller's Proctor is more fiction than fact.

Meserve, Walter J. "*The Crucible*: 'This Fool and I.'" In *Arthur Miller: New Perspectives,* edited by Robert A. Martin, 127–38. Englewood Cliffs: Prentice-Hall, 1982. An original and intelligent essay by a respected drama scholar.

Morgan, Edmund S. "Arthur Miller's *The Crucible* and the Salem Witch Trials: A Historian's View." In *The Golden and Brazen World: Papers in Literature and History 1650–1800,* edited by John M. Wallace, 171–86. Berkeley: University of California Press, 1985. Speaking as the Puritans' advocate, draws a picture of seventeenth-century Puritanism different than that in the play.

Morley, Sheridan. "*The Crucible*." *Playbill: The National Theatre Magazine,* 31 July 1990, 64–65. Interesting comments on the occasion of the play's London revival celebrating Miller's seventy-fifth birthday.

O'Neal, Michael J. "History, Myth, and Name Magic in Arthur Miller's *The Crucible*." *CLIO* 12, no. 2 (Winter 1983): 111–22. Suggests that the play's success rests on a sequence of discernible stages in Proctor's moral development.

Porter, Thomas E. "The Long Shadow of the Law: *The Crucible*." In *Myth and Modern Drama,* 177–99. Detroit: Wayne State University Press, 1969. Reprinted in Martine, 75–92. Remains among the most suggestive chapters written on the play.

Styan, J. L. "A View From the Crucible; or, The Compleat Playwright." *Michigan Quarterly Review* 18 (1979): 509–15. Title may be misleading on this interesting review of Miller's *Theater Essays*.

Walker, Philip. "Arthur Miller's *The Crucible*: Tragedy or Allegory?" *Western Speech* 20 (1956): 222–24. Sees the play as a dramatic allegory on McCarthyism but suggests that it is not fully achieved as either personal tragedy or political allegory.

Warshow, Robert. "The Liberal Conscience in *The Crucible*." In *Arthur Miller: A Collection of Critical Essays,* edited by Robert W. Corrigan. 111–21.

Englewood Cliffs: Prentice-Hall, 1969. A celebrated assault on the play and its author; examines the relationship between the events at Salem and those of the 1950s.

Bibliographies

Eissenstat, Martha Turnquist. "Arthur Miller: A Bibliography." *Modern Drama* 5 (May 1962): 93–106. A good if dated bibliography.

Ferres, John H. *Arthur Miller: A Reference Guide.* Boston: G. K. Hall, 1979. An excellent and comprehensive volume that includes intelligent summary abstracts of each item of writing about Miller between 1944 and 1977.

Hayashi, Tetsumaro. *An Index to Arthur Miller Criticism,* 2d ed. Metuchen, N.J.: Scarecrow, 1976. A most ambitious guide to scholarship; concludes with a bibliography of bibliographies on Miller. Appendix lists and locates unpublished manuscripts and letters by Miller.

Jensen, George H. *Arthur Miller: A Bibliographic Checklist.* Columbia, S.C.: Faust, 1976. Includes reproductions of title pages and a publishing history of Miller's works.

Ungar, Harriet. "The Writings of and about Arthur Miller: A Checklist 1936–1967." *Bulletin of the New York Public Library* 74 (1970): 107–34. Thorough, if now dated.

Index

The Author

James J. Martine, professor of English at St. Bonaventure University, has published numerous books and articles. His books include *Fred Lewis Pattee and American Literature* (1973), a two-volume *Student Guide to American Literature* (1977), *Critical Essays on Arthur Miller* (1979), and *Critical Essays on Eugene O'Neill* (1984). He has edited three volumes of the *Dictionary of Literary Biography* (1981), those devoted to American novelists 1910–45; and the first volume in the Contemporary Authors Bibliography Series, that on *American Novelists* (1986). He has published essays on Ernest Hemingway, F. Scott Fitzgerald, Thomas Wolfe, Joseph Heller, Eugene O'Neill, Arthur Miller, Lanford Wilson, and the history of American literature. His work has also been published in the *American Literary Almanac* (1988). The thing he likes best, however, is teaching undergraduate classes at St. Bonaventure.